What readers are saying about

The Journey...Beyond Shallow Waters --

Staying true to the course, fighting the good fight of faith, and never giving up along our journey is what our objective and mission in this life should be.
The Journey....Beyond Shallow Waters by Teresa L. Colbert is very purposeful, a delight to read and will help strengthen your faith and walk with God. The shared stories offer hope and inspiration in such a practical way that every reader can relate. There is a chosen path He has selected for everyone, and our mission and work is to get there. This book will speak volumes to your heart.

Treva R. Gordon, Author of *Leading Ladies*
President / CCS Publications

"Captivated by the author's profound insight—Teresa took my hand and escorted me beyond shallow waters. In the deep waters, I encountered such hope and witnessed something beautiful coming out of something so painful."

Jackie Kendall, bestselling author of *Lady in Waiting* and President of Power to Grow, Inc.

The Journey...Beyond Shallow Waters is indeed an exciting read. Readers will not only be engaged, but many will be able to see reflections of their own lives within these pages. Like Ry'ah, they too will realize that God has a plan and purpose for their lives.
I'm ready to venture *Beyond Shallow Waters.*

Victor C. Hall, M.Ed, *Author of Soul Food...4U*

The Journey...Beyond Shallow Waters will engulf and take the reader on a journey that defies human understanding and belief. Get ready to be immersed into Ry'ah's life and into the walk of faith she dared to take.

This book, written by Teresa Colbert, is one of excitement, faith, and trying new things. I am honored to know such a beautiful, humble, sold out Christian woman who not only speaks with anointing but writes with anointing and conviction.

Danielle Atkinson, Author of *You Made Me Beautiful*

In *The Journey...Beyond Shallow Waters*, Teresa establishes herself as a gifted writer. She takes the reader on a tumultuous faith-filled journey of her richly developed character, Ry'ah. The story of Ry'ah's life is told in such a way that it will keep the reader glued to the pages. I could not stop reading a word of this, no matter who kept calling my name. It left me wanting more (the true sign of a good book)!

Jenn Hall, Instructor, Department of Kinesiology and Health, Georgia State University, Atlanta, GA and Creator of *LTS LeBarre.*

The Journey...

Beyond Shallow

Waters

To: Julie Sather

Teresa L. Colbert

Jesus Never changes!

Teresa L. Colbert

The Journey...Beyond Shallow Waters
Published by Yawn's Publishing
198 North Street
Canton, GA 30114
www.yawnsbooks.com

Library of Congress Control Number: 2013911159

ISBN: 978-1-936815-90-6 paperback
       978-1-936815-91-3 eBook

Printed in the United States

Acknowledgements

To Aunt Carolyn:

You were the first "Life Speaker" declaring this book, while it was yet underway, as a best seller! The late nights wherein we shared laughter, heartache, advice and prayer are ones I will always treasure. Thank you for encouraging me and believing in this project. Thank you for embracing and sharing the memories of this incredible journey. I pause to ask you the question you always ended our phone conversations with, "Do you know how much I love you?"

Marcia:

Every journey is enriched when two walk together in agreement. Ruth followed Naomi. Paul traveled with Silas. Jonathan defended David and I can't imagine what this journey would have been without your faithful prayers, constant encouragement and your servant's heart. I will forever be eternally grateful for the sacrifices you've made with me along this journey.

The *"We Walkers"*:

This journey has been all the more special because of you. Together we have walked through the fires of persecution, stood in the midst of opposition, upheld each other in times of crisis and rejoiced in victories. You have unequivocally embraced me with the love of Christ. Your faithful prayers, without question, have reached heaven on my behalf. I am both humbled and honored to be called your sister in Christ.

To Jesus, the Author and Finisher of my faith:

The One who calls and continues to challenge me to take my "net" of faith into deeper waters, words alone can't express my love and devotion. My hope is that sometime along the way, there have been moments wherein I have brought a trickle of joy to your heart and a smile to your face. I can't imagine living this life without you...wow! What a journey! I know the best is yet to come! If I may borrow the words from the psalmist to convey my heart to you: *"Whom have I in heaven but You? And there is none upon earth that I desire besides You."* (Psalm 73:25)

Contents

"Do not fear the winds of adversity. Remember a kite rises against the wind rather than with it."

Unknown

An Ember
of Promise!

It has been said, "*Without a vision, the people perish*". Far too many dreams lay like smoldering embers in these Appalachian Mountains, struggling to be rekindled by the slightest wind of hope. Perhaps they would be awakened by the gentle breeze of the east wind promising the dawning of a new day. Or maybe they would be ignited by the warm, south wind bringing with it the expectation of a pleasant life. So they waited in anticipation and days turned to months, and months into years. Oh yes, the winds came and they came often. But contrary to what was hoped for, these winds did not beget gentleness; yield any pleasantries or the dawning of a promising future. One by one, their hopes were blasted by the bitter cold winds of adversity; and one by one, the embers faded, yielding to the brutal winds.

Ry'ah awakened before dawn, somewhat startled by a crashing thud and the throbbing in her right foot. As the rain beat steadily against the windows, her mind raced while she tried to make some sense of her seemingly muddled state. Her drowsy eyes roamed in search of familiarity, but the subdued shadows of the darkened room presented only obscure answers. As she stood, the creaking of her grandmother's rocking chair added to the unsettling arousal. Within moments, obscurity gave way to the nippy air of the early autumn morning, clearing the cobwebs from her brain.

Wincing with each step, Ry'ah gingerly made her way over to the fireplace. It had been a spectacular evening, an idyllic way to finish off yet another riveting novel. The fire had taken center stage, displaying its theatrics of dancing flames, glowing embers and crackling sounds. She sat for hours mesmerized by its performing silhouettes before finally succumbing to its beguiling warmth. She'd missed the curtain call. The show had ended and now she stood shivering before a sleeping heap of ashes.

With dogged determination, Ry'ah prodded until finally, from beneath the heaps of extinguished embers, emerged one small cinder. Peering through a cocoon of dense ash, the cinder blushed refusing to give up, aglow with promise.

3

Repeated attempts of blowing coaxed it into flame, upon which Ry'ah squealed with delight, "An ember of promise!" The words seemed to linger like a never ending echo: "An ember of promise, an ember of promise, an ember of promise, an ember of promise!" Was this some sort of an epiphany, perhaps?

Indeed, a fire remained within and with it a promise of rekindling, a pledge of renewal and the rebirth of a dream. Lying dormant, the faint ember would soon join those that had gone before it. It was yet another confirmation. Running her fingers through her hair and down the back of her neck, Ry'ah contemplated the choices that lie before her. Would she resign herself to the fears and the "what if's," allowing her dreams to die in these Appalachian Mountains? Or would her faith lead her to go in search of her destiny?

For months she had been keenly aware that soon she would say goodbye to the wonderful place she had called home for twenty-plus years. She had grown accustomed to the small town community lifestyle, where merchants greeted their customers by name. The locals were friendly and caring enough to know their neighbors, and family members found reasons to gather together for any occasion. But the fire of her faith burned from within. There was no denying the inward pull, as the words once again emerged from her lips, "an ember of promise."

Ry'ah was known for having a good head on her shoulders, never causing any trouble and being easy to get along with. Although she steeled herself to withstand the impending skepticism, the stinging tears streamed as the harsh words spewed forth: "religious fanatic," "she's always been a little 'different'", and other brusque comments. "Would she really leave her family, her friends, a steady job and move to a strange city with no job prospects, and no family support? Who in their right mind does that?"

Despite their cynicism, Ry'ah was absolutely certain of the Word. The instruction she had received was from God. Maybe one day...she hoped, maybe one day...they would come to

5

understand, but now she would heed the still small voice that was:

- Leading her away from her comfort zone to become better acquainted with *The Comforter.*
- Leading her away from shallow religion to an intimate relationship with the *Lover of her soul.*
- Leading her away from all she thought she knew to a life of discipleship with *The Teacher.*

With pen in hand, Ry'ah struggled. Words failed her. How do I say goodbye? How can I explain the unexplainable? The answer came from within: ...invite them to come along.

Dear Friend,

I welcome you to join me on the most remarkable excursion, adventuresome journey, and life-changing encounter to which I have been beckoned. Accompany me as we meander through the valleys of uncertainties, climb mountains of un-

foreseen challenges and forge through waters of unpredictability. Don't bail yet, my friend. To really capture and appreciate this wonder-filled experience, you must stay the course. Yes, it is quite possible we will venture into unfamiliar territory, but not to worry, for we have an experienced Guide who will be leading the way. He will supply all of your needs for the journey. So if you should tire along the way, we'll stop and rest beside quiet waters. If you should become hungry, I assure you, He has plenty of bread to satisfy and sustain you for the journey. Not quite convinced? Still contemplating as to whether or not to join me? Need a little more persuasion? Then imagine yourself licking the spoon, smelling the tantalizing aroma and then refusing a slice of a triple-layered chocolate cake! Or declining free front row seats to a sold-out game of your favorite team, preferring to spend the day cleaning out gutters. How about choosing popcorn and a movie in lieu of a four week, all expenses paid vacation to any destination of your choice in the world? Are you kidding me!!!? Would you r-e-a-l-l-y forfeit such treasures? Of course NOT!

So I implore you my friend, please do not decline this invitation. Don't refuse this opportunity or pass up this unforgettable experience. Don't miss the exhilarating surprises that await you as you reach the summit of the arduous climbs, the unspeakable joys that spill forth as you conquer the tempestuous storms in uncharted waters, the pleasure

of basking in welcoming rays of triumph
as you emerge from lonely, obscure
valleys. The Guide is waiting. There is
only one requirement: be sure to stay
close to Him, for He knows the way.

Your friend,

Ry'ah

Come. Take this journey with Ry'ah.

"Faith never knows where it is being led, but it knows and loves the One who is leading."

Oswald Chambers

The Journey

Everything has a starting place. *"In the beginning, God created the heavens and the earth". (Genesis 1:1)* Ships set sail from the dock; Olympic runners sprint from the starting blocks; planes take off from the runway; racehorses bound from the gate; trains leave the station; paintings emerge from blank canvases, and mighty oaks grow from small acorns. Well, my journey began in the mountains of North Carolina. Ever been there? No, then place it on your bucket list. You'll be in for a treat as you experience the breathtaking waterfalls, occasional sightings of a mother bear with her cubs, deer grazing in open fields, meadows of beautiful wildflowers, white water rapids, stunning arrays of autumn colors, wintry snowcapped mountains and quaint small towns.

It was in one of those small towns that I was born and raised, as the town folk would say. The locals are usually welcoming and quite friendly once they smoke you over. Not to worry my friend, this is just the old timers' way of getting acquainted with you. So I invite you to return with me; walk with me; laugh with me; cry with me and rejoice with me as I recall those stirring, yet formidable memories.

Do you see the yellow house, the one with the white shutters as we crest the top of the hill? That's the house in which I grew up. You are welcome to come in, but I must tell you my childhood home may not be like yours. I won't be able to offer you home baked cookies or lemonade, and you may find the house unkempt. You won't smell fresh brewed coffee, but another strong beverage I'm sure you'll recognize. Oh that guy? No, he's not my dad. He's what you might refer to as a *live-in*. Excuse me for not introducing him, but during those years I erased him. Let me briefly explain. I am a pencil with an eraser, and he is a mistake, an error in judgment, someone who wasn't meant to be in my life or in her life. As a child, I did not have the power or the authority to physically remove him from our lives; so I erased him from my mind. Oh sure, he ate our food, watched our television and stayed at our house; but in order to endure his presence, I mentally and emotionally erased him. He wasn't important to me; he contributed nothing to my life and we rarely conversed, which is what I preferred. But enough about him...he isn't relevant to the reason for my return. Come on in and meet her, my Mother.

Two-Sided Coin

Dear Friend,

Oftentimes something of value can be so well-hidden by the pain of life, that if prejudged too quickly, we may miss an amazing opportunity to discover its true worth. For every now and then, priceless treasures are discovered in the most remarkable places.

Lodged within a cracked clay pot, the encrusted coin longed to be discovered and appreciated for its value. Deemed problematic as it lay amidst the shards and believed to be worthless, the coin remained out of view. Intense scrutiny revealed years of wear and abuse. The coin, which had seen better days, now lacked its original luster and was in need of tender loving care.

My sisters and I were parented by a single mother whose broken heart and shattered dreams oftentimes caused her to weep and wail. She cursed and cried as she drank to escape the pain and the misery of a life in which she had lost hope. As a child, I often wondered what had transpired in her life to cause her to drown her sorrows in hard liquor. What lies had the enemy of her soul whispered, convincing her to continue this downward spiral? What living nightmare haunted her and replayed in her mind daily? Had she ever known real peace? Like a driver ignoring the warning signs posted, "Bridge Out" and rapidly increasing the speed, she seemed to disregard the doctor's reports warning that continual, habitual drinking would inevitably lead to cirrhosis of the liver or worse. *The thief does not come except to steal, and to kill, and to destroy.* (John 10:10) He was determined to kill her spirit, steal her dreams and destroy her body. As a child I observed helplessly while he purposely continued his mission.

One of my most heartbreaking memories was sitting for hours in the hospital room watching helplessly as my mother suffered through detoxification. Hearing her screams, hallucinations, and seeing her in restraints was unbearable. Yet, I was trusting God would hear my simple tearstained prayer, "Please help her!"

I was twelve-years-old. Hospital rules were much more lax then. I can't imagine a child being subjected to such a traumatic ordeal in today's society. My mother was "really sick" I was told numerous times by a preacher, the hospital custodian and my grandmother who were the only visitors who stopped by for brief moments. Oddly enough though, none of her "friends", her drinking buddies, ever came by. Neither did the live-in boyfriend. My mother was thirty-four-years-old and life had already taken a cruel toll on her. The drinking binges would last for about three days, mostly occurring over the weekends.

For many years of my life, I dreaded Fridays as the quiet school week ended. The school bus promptly arrived in front of our house at 3:45 p.m. and I never quite knew what embarrassing episode to expect when I exited the bus. Would she be waiting at the bus stop with a beer in hand, staggering around in the front yard, or swearing loudly at one of the neighbors?

My junior high school years were also somewhat disappointing. Remember those fun weekend slumber parties held at Lindsay's house where they were staying up all night and watching movies? Remember the next weekend at Lacey's house for her 14th birthday? Remember the following weekend at Debbie's house, attending the Homecoming football game on Friday night and then going out for pizza afterwards? Remember Stephanie's house the next weekend

19

with a bonfire and roasting marshmallows? I was never able to "make it" to those slumber parties. Oh yes, I was invited. But I knew if I attended, eventually my friends would wonder why the party was never at my house. And that could never happen because slumber parties are held on the weekends! How could I explain to them the parties held at my house were off-limits to young adolescent silly girls? How do you begin to tell your friends your house smelled like beer, not baked cookies? I thought it best our friendship remain at school, and the secret of my alcoholic mother would remain with me.

However, my friend Melinda inadvertently happened upon my well-kept secret while passing through the community where I lived. She told me about "a woman" whom she and her brother had seen staggering about and was obviously drunk. They had to swerve into the other lane to keep from hitting her and the woman proceeded to yell curse words at them. Melinda wondered if I knew the woman. So I said what a typical adolescent, who was ashamed and afraid of exposing a family

20

secret to a classmate would have said, "No." Somehow in my mind, I justified my answer. There were at least two other women in the community who suffered from alcohol abuse. So, it was possible the woman my friend described could have been Ms. Loretta or Ms. LeAnn, but some-how I knew it was most likely my mother.

Oh how I wished Melinda had passed by our house on Monday through Thursday when things were normal and life was so much better. For then, she would have seen an entirely different woman, a woman I would have happily acknowledged, not shamefully denied. If Melinda had only come during the week, I would have gladly invited her into our home where she would have seen:

- My mother was sober and neatly dressed.

- She was not loud and obnoxious, but quiet and in control.

- On rare occasions she could be heard whistling hymns.

- Our house was clean and there was no stench of alcohol.
- My mother was a good cook and dinner was ready promptly at five o' clock.
- We watched family television programs together each evening.
- Homework and chores were done and bedtime was 9:00 p.m.

It was true, now I think about it. I didn't know this woman Melinda saw. Yes, I lived with her but I didn't know her.

"When I was a child, I spoke as a child; I understood as a child, I thought as a child". (1 Corinthians 13:11) And I was an obedient child.

So when my mother declared, "You do as I say, not as I do", that's what I did. Whenever her friends arrived on Friday evenings, my sister and I played outside or elsewhere within the community.

On weekends, we were allowed to stay up past our weekday bedtime since the party sometimes lasted until around midnight. I remember awakening on Saturday and Sunday mornings to the stench of alcohol, empty beer cans strewn about the living room, ashtrays overflowing with cigarette butts, a deck of cards from the previous night's poker game, loose change and liquor glasses left on the coffee table, and the occasional friend who drank too much and passed out on the sofa. After my mother washed down a *Goody* powder with a *Coca Cola* (this was her antidote for a hangover); we began the cleaning and airing out of the house. While emptying ashtrays, sweeping the floor, washing liquor glasses, and placing beer cans in the garbage, I always remained quiet, fighting back tears of anger, resentment, disappointment and helplessness.

Although this weekly cycle remained the same for many years, I never quite adapted. The Friday afternoon disappointments, the shame, the hope "this weekend" would be different, continued as did my genuine love for my mother. There were so many things I didn't understand and so many questions I dared not ask but internalized and in my young and inexperienced mind tried to rationalize. Why was she so sad? Who or what had hurt her so deeply that she oftentimes sobbed uncontrollably? Why does she drink so much? Do we always have to wait for the welfare check to arrive? Why does her boyfriend live at our house? Why does he always get angry and hit her?

God was the only "safe person" to whom I could direct these questions, not out loud, just silently. I wasn't really expecting any answers. It was just comforting to know it was safe to ask, to ponder, and somehow I knew He cared and He loved us. He even loved my mother, who many times during her drunken stupors would curse using His name. Many judged her and others pitied her. But I loved her! To be fair, there are always two sides to every coin. So please allow me to share with you the other side of my mother, a side rarely seen by many, but one I will always treasure.

Have you ever witnessed the protectiveness of a mother bear towards her cubs? She does whatever is necessary to keep them out of harm's way, even if it means putting herself in danger. My mother was a petite woman who would champion anyone who dared to threaten or harm her children. Her live-in boyfriend was never permitted to discipline us in any way. His teasing, which irritated me, was also forbidden by her.

She made it absolutely clear in a threatening tone, "we were her kids, period, and if he didn't like it, then leave." More accurately, she said, "Then, get the hell out!"

Living in a small town, there wasn't much to do in the way of entertainment. Oh sure, we had a movie theater, a skating rink, the Lion's Club swimming pool, a bowling alley, and a few fast food restaurants (all requiring money), but one of the main attractions for kids was the carnival during the latter part of August. There never seemed to be any money left over after the welfare check was used to pay utilities and other household bills, but my mother always made sure my sister and I were able to attend the carnival. We were given ten dollars each and we could choose to spend all or part of it. My mother waited patiently while we rode the carousel, the scrambler, the swings and the Ferris wheel. Then, we played a few games in the hopes of winning a stuffed animal or some other toy prize. Before leaving the park, we bought cotton candy, candied apples and a bag of popcorn. Together we walked home contented, all the while munching on popcorn.

At times, my mother worked for Dr. & Mrs. Mahoney doing odd jobs (light housekeeping, babysitting and cleaning his office). I was thrilled whenever I got to tag along. I loved to read and I was fascinated with the volumes of books, science magazines and encyclopedias at the Mahoney's house. Imagine my surprise and delight when I came home from school to find stacks of prior issues of National Wildlife magazines on my bed! *Are you beginning to see why I loved and*

appreciated the "other side of the coin"?
Then stay with me, there's more.

One evening, an encyclopedia salesman knocked on our door. My first thought was, "Mister, you've got the wrong house!" But then, my mother came out of the kitchen and to my surprise she invited him to sit down and she listened to his sales pitch. The encyclopedias were obviously much too expensive for a family on welfare, but the salesman went on to explain a doable 24-month payment plan. He opened the box and handed me a dark green A-B volume of the Encyclopedia Britannica series. I dared not hope for these.

After all, I was used to using the ones at the library. The long and short of it, you guessed it! Several weeks later boxes of new encyclopedias arrived at our house, and oh how I treasured them for many years. I often wondered if she had used the extra money she earned from the Mahoney's, or cashed in an insurance policy, or won the money in a poker game. I never asked how she did it. I just thanked her.

Although my mother seemed to have lost her drive and ambition, she constantly found the words to encourage me. They were words of life and hope. "You're going to make it, Reese!" (This was her nickname for me.) I didn't know what she meant at that time, but these words gave me aspirations, and the determination to reach for my dreams. They began to shape who I would become. She encouraged me to excel in my studies. A's and B's were the only grades she would accept, and B's were questionable. Usually my report cards consisted of A's and the one B+. She beamed with pride as she told her friends about my achievements. I learned from my grandmother that my mother had once been an excellent student and was promoted and even skipped a grade. That's another one of those unknown areas of her life that I would have liked to have been privy to. What were her favorite subjects? What was her favorite book? What had been her dreams? What had caused her dreams to die?

Other surprises I happened upon...she and Dr. Mahoney had been friends and playmates as children. As she called my name during roll call, my 5th grade English teacher, Mrs. Thompson, revealed that she and my mother had been best friends. She went on to say that my mother was a very intelligent woman, and she was sure I would be one of her best students! My mother confirmed Mrs. Thompson's story and was happy to know she would be my teacher. I didn't know whether to feel shocked or pressured or both!

There are many episodes of my life I wish I could change, rewrite or omit during the spring of my senior year in high school. After a cold harsh winter with an unusual amount of heavy snowfall, the warm days of spring finally arrived. The birds were chirping, flowers blooming, trees blossoming and two exciting events were soon to occur in a matter of weeks: my high school prom and graduation! To add to these momentous occasions, my mother had agreed to attend my

29

graduation ceremony. Yes, this was a big deal for me.

For the past few years, my sister and I had been living with my grandmother. My mother's drinking had escalated beyond the weekend binges. The social worker visited our home during one of those "times" and observed the aftermath of a weekend party. Documentation of my mother's bloodshot eyes, the smell of alcohol, slurred speech, unkempt appearance and untidy house, no doubt made their way into the social worker's file and soon thereafter, my sister and I went to live with my grandmother. "It was for the best," we were told. Even though I lived with my grandmother, my mother continued to monitor my grades, social activities, and was involved in any disciplinary action required. Although she never attended any of my track meets or scholastic awards ceremonies, she agreed to come to my graduation and I was thrilled!

Using some of the money I earned from my part-time job, I purchased a pants suit for her. In her younger days my mother had been a stylish woman, but over the years she seemed most comfortable in slacks and a blouse. The pants suit fit perfectly on her petite frame and my eyes glistened as I envisioned the special day we would celebrate together!

It was a hot Sunday afternoon. The high school parking lot was steadily filling up; the auditorium was buzzing with activity, and the soon-to-be graduates were excitedly chatting with classmates and signing each other's yearbooks. The orchestra was warming up while family members were streaming in. It was graduation day! I scanned the auditorium trying to get a glimpse of my mother. I saw my grandmother and others, but where was she? The orchestra began to play; graduates were escorted into the auditorium and school officials gave their declarations. Heartwarming invocations and speeches were given, and then the receiving of the diplomas began. The auditorium erupted in applause, and the senior class received their diplomas, cheered loudly and tossed their caps into the air! While hugging teachers and

31

classmates, we made our way out of the auditorium and onto the lawn.

In the sea of graduation gowns and caps, I saw her. She had come! The day I had long awaited and excitedly anticipated, the day I had envisioned sharing with her was finally here. As I approached her, waves of disappointment, embarrassment and heartache welled up within me. Why? I screamed silently. She had been sober for weeks, so why not today, of all days? Why hadn't she worn the new pants suit? Why hadn't she styled her hair? Why did the stench of alcohol invade what was supposed to be one of the happiest days of my life?

This is an episode I would like to rewrite. The only existing proof of that episode is captured in a single photo displayed in my sister's home. Actually, there are only two photos of my mother and me of which I am aware. One is of her holding me as baby. She is beautifully dressed in a stylish suit and probably wearing Jean Nate', her favorite perfume. The photo must have been taken on a Sunday afternoon or on some special occasion because I was wearing a dress and a matching bonnet. I have a copy and would proudly show this picture. She appears to be healthy and in "a good place". The other photo is the one taken at my graduation.

As I write about this segment of my life, a revelation has occurred regarding these photos. My mother strongly disliked having her picture taken, but on two occasions she willingly had her picture taken and both times her picture was taken with me. I am amazed it has taken over thirty years for this fact to resonate with me. The absolute truth of the matter is, whether she was sober or not, her love for me never wavered. She was proud of my accomplishments, and she kept her promise of attending my graduation to me. My mother knew she was sick, but I wonder if she knew just how sick she really was. If so, that was another one of those topics she never discussed with me.

And though my graduation day was one I wish I could rewrite, the following week is one I wish I could have eliminated altogether.

33

It was early Saturday morning when my grandmother answered a knock at the door. My mother's boyfriend was concerned that he could not awaken her, and he thought something was terribly wrong. I jumped up, pulled on clothes over my pajamas and sprinted to her house. My bounding into the house had not stirred her, for she was lying in the bed. I called out to her and when there was no response, I slapped her on the face hoping to arouse her. She was warm to the touch, so I assumed she was in a coma. Ms. Kilpatrick, a neighbor, called the ambulance and agreed to stay with her while I went to notify my oldest sister. When we returned, we were told my mother had passed away. As we made funeral arrangements, the next few days seemed like a bad dream that I desperately wanted to awaken from. Life seemed so unfair! Within two weeks, I had danced at my high school prom, graduated from high school and was now burying my mother.

Was it my fault? Guilt overtook me like a dense fog resting on a mountain lake. How long would this gut-wrenching secret continue to haunt

34

me? I have heard it said, "Be careful what you pray for."

Weeks prior to her death, there had been yet another weekend "episode" at my mother's house. There were several variations to the "story", but in short, my mother's body had taken another blow. The black eye, swollen face and broken ribs screamed of physical abuse, but the fact finding mission was hampered by "the good 'ole boys" lies and loyalty. A few claimed they didn't see anything (although they were in the house)! "He" alleged she was drunk and fell off the porch. Neighbors said they overheard loud arguing. Someone else claimed the "live-in" hit her and then she staggered and fell. She was in excruciating pain and said nothing. I knew her well enough to know that whatever had happened, this would not be the end of it. She was silently planning, waiting and plotting her next move. Her opponent had struck, but in due time when he least expected it, she would make sure he remembered well the pain he inflicted.

Once, I remember her telling my sister who was taunted by a bully, "Whenever you fight someone bigger and stronger than you, you don't fight fair. You fight to win!"

Feeling so angry, torn and the need to be alone, I retreated to a private spot on a hillside and tearfully cried out to God. "She's forty-years-old. She's been through enough. Will she continue to live in hell and then die and go to hell? I'd rather you go ahead and take her... She can't go through this again.... Please Lord, I'd rather you take her... If you take her, at least she would have some peace!" Oh if she could only have some good days... happy days.... peaceful days, and if not here on this earth, then surely in the presence of a loving, heavenly Father.

My prayer was answered, and now I struggled with the guilt. I held it all together during the funeral service, trying to be strong and a comfort to my sisters. But at the gravesite...the somber faces... "ashes to ashes, dust to dust"....the casket that held my mother's body suspended over an open grave, waiting to be lowered ...NO!

... Please, No! I didn't get to say goodbye! Oh, God please don't take her! I didn't mean it!

Now what? What do I do? I was eighteen-years-old facing an uncertain future. According to my grandmother, she and my mom had had numerous conversations weeks before her death. My grandmother was the beneficiary of her insurance policies. The instructions were explicit. After all expenses were paid, all remaining monies were to be used for my college education.

Many years later, as I looked back over those unsettling years to those unexplained episodes, those shameful occurrences, my heavenly Father has graciously given me insight and understanding. Replacing all of those childhood doubts, He has reassured me of my self-worth and purpose. He's filtered the facts of my life and illuminated them with truth:

Yes, it was a fact I was conceived as a result of a "night of passion", and born out of wedlock. Yes, fornication is a sin. But my birth was not a mistake.

37

"Before I formed you in the womb I knew you; Before you were born I sanctified you..." (Jeremiah 1:5) *"For you formed my inward parts; you covered me in my mother's womb. My frame was not hidden from you, when I was made in secret, and skillfully wrought in the lowest parts of the earth. Your eyes saw my unformed body."* (Psalm 139: 13, 15)

I am not a "love child" as the world may say, but I am a Loved Child.

"...Yes I have loved you with an everlasting love...," says the Lord. (Jeremiah 31:3)

My future would not be haunted by those daunting episodes of my childhood.

"For I know the thoughts that I think toward you, says the LORD, thoughts of peace and not of evil, to give you a future and a hope." (Jeremiah 29:11)

What about my mother? Had God seen anything good and valuable in her broken life?

As I searched the pages of His written word, I found other women who once lived sordid lives and in whom God loved and found purpose:

- Rahab, a prostitute who saved Joshua and the Israelite spies from death. (Joshua 2) She, too, is part of Jesus' lineage.
- Bathsheba committed adultery with King David and became the mother of King Solomon.   (2 Samuel 11)
- The Samaritan woman who had five husbands. She too had a "live-in" boyfriend and her life was changed after meeting Jesus. (John 4)
- The woman "caught in adultery."

> *"When Jesus had raised Himself up and saw no one but the woman, He said to her, "Woman, where are those accusers of yours? Has no one condemned you?"*
>
> *She said, "No one, Lord."*

And Jesus said to her, "Neither do I condemn you; go and sin no more." (John 8:10-11)

I grieved so after my mother's death, wondering if she had made peace with God during her final day, her final hours. I prayed earnestly to God for an answer and one night in a dream, I saw her dressed in a simple white gown. The wind was blowing and she was whistling the tune of the song "Amazing Grace".

I have come to realize whether a coin is shiny or dirty, old or new, found on the street, lodged in a broken vessel or encased in a collector's box, it has worth. So dear friend, if you should happen upon a dirty coin, don't hastily toss it aside. Take a closer look and you will find it more valuable than first thought.

Oh yes my Friend, God can and does take broken lives and somehow by His grace redeems them.

"...For man looks at the outward appearance, but the LORD looks at the heart." (1 Samuel 16:7)

"Goodbyes are not forever.

Goodbyes are not the end.

They simply mean I'll miss you, until we meet

again!"

Unknown

So Long, Farewell

Dear Friend,

Do you recall as a child being sent to bed on Christmas Eve? You've put on your pajamas, brushed your teeth, said goodnight, and now you are lying in bed looking up at the ceiling. Remember? The tossing, the turning, the adrenaline, maybe a drink of water, a final trip to the bathroom, glancing at the clock and sighing as it shows 10:30!

Will this night ever end? "Christmas Eve," ah a night filled with excitement and sleeplessness, wondering what the morning would bring.

For weeks the anticipation had grown and tomorrow... yes finally tomorrow... You do remember, don't you?

It was those similar feelings of exhilaration and anticipation that stirred within me one particular night while lying in bed. Confirmation from God's word and an inner knowing assured me I was about to embark on the most amazing and incredible journey. Like a balloon about to burst, I excitedly posed the question to God out loud. "I wonder where I'm going." And while he didn't give me all of the answers, He did give me a measure of faith ... enough to step out.

I was on a quest to personally know more about this God in whom I had placed my faith. I wanted to know if my life had purpose and specifically the plans He had in mind for me. So I went obediently...I went excitedly...I went naively...I went expectantly.

Obediently -- "...and the sheep hear His voice; and He calls His own sheep by name and leads them out. And when He brings out His own sheep, He goes before them; and the sheep follow Him, for they know His voice." (John 10:3-4)

Excitedly – *"...Follow Me, and I will make you fishers of men." They immediately left their nets and followed Him."* (Matthew 4:19-20)

Naively – *"By faith Abraham obeyed when he was called to go out to the place which he would receive as an inheritance. And he went out, not knowing where he was going."* (Hebrews 11:8)

Expectantly – *"Now faith is the substance of things hoped for, the evidence of things not seen."* (Hebrews 11:1) *"Ask, and it will be given to you; seek, and you will find; knock, and it will be opened to you."* (Matthew 7:7)

So I went asking, seeking and knocking unto Him who had the answers. I was determined to knock until doors were opened, to seek until I found answers, to ask until I received all He would reveal to me.

Like Abraham, I was to go to a place I knew not. Like Abraham, I would learn to walk by faith and not by sight.

"So Abram departed as the LORD had spoken to him, and Lot went with him." (Genesis 12:4)

• So I departed as the Lord had directed me, but unlike Abraham, no family members accompanied me.

"And Abram was seventy-five years old when he departed from Haran." (Genesis 12:4)

• I was single and in my mid-twenties.

"Then Abram took Sarai his wife and Lot his brother's son, and all their possessions that they had gathered, and the people whom they had acquired in Haran, and they departed to go to the land of Canaan." (Genesis 12: 5)

• Taking only college and auto loans, meager belongings and an assured faith, I left behind the small close-knit community which I had known as "home."

Was I really comparing my journey to Abraham's? That was absurd! Or maybe not, after all, we shared one distinct commonality:

FAITH... we believed God.

Teresa L. Colbert

"Growth means change and change involves risk, stepping from the known to the unknown."

Author unknown

I'm here. I arrived safely. There are so many emotions swirling around inside of me, I feel like a helicopter preparing for takeoff.

How can one be excited, scared, apprehensive, relieved, and peaceful all at once?

Maybe I will feel more at "home," once these boxes are unpacked. Wow! That has a weird sound to it, calling a strange place, "home." And yet, it feels, it feels right!

Teresa L. Colbert

So, Now What?

It had been a few months and still no job offers. My bank account was in grave danger of insufficient funds. Had it really come to this? After graduating from college, I prided myself in maintaining a steady job, building a savings account, meeting my financial obligations, and occasionally rewarding myself with a vacation, a fun weekend with friends or a shopping excursion.

My life was sailing along comfortably, safely, and I was anticipating a bright future, never imagining one day I would venture into these unfamiliar waters. Waves of questioning, reasoning and second-guessing continued to roll in like the ocean tide. What was I thinking? Should I have remained in the shallow waters of familiarity? Was I crazy to leave the safe waters of reassurance, and predictability? Out here the waters were much deeper. Panic swelled as I began to focus on currents of uncertainty, periods of isolation and fear of the unknown. Would I drown? Was I in over my head? Would I ever know the familiarity of the shallow waters again?

How long would I drift in these strange, cold, intimidating waters?

Yes, I was scared, very scared, but certain I was led here to these deeper waters and in "due time", God would reveal his plan and purpose.

Never having been one to settle for "that's just the way things are" and having a tenacity for acquiring answers, I went straight to the Source. Since God had led me here, I wanted to know, needed to know why. Thus, I cried out to Him for answers. After all, He did say to, *"Ask,"* and *"Seek,"* didn't He? (Matthew 7:7) The answers I sought were found embedded in His written word.

"Then He got into one of the boats, which was Simon's, and asked him to put out a little from the shore. And He sat down and taught the multitudes from the boat. When He had stopped speaking, He said to Simon, "Launch out into the deep and let down your nets for a catch." But Simon answered and said to Him, "Master, we have toiled all night and caught nothing; nevertheless, at your word I will let down the net." (Luke 5:3-5)

"Lord what are you saying to me through this passage of scripture?" I asked. Within my spirit, I heard these words:

"Ry'ah, you have been in shallow waters too long. You have been where all is too familiar to you: your family, your community, your church. I want to take the net of your faith into deeper waters."

Still not quite sure as to what He meant exactly, I submitted and said, "Okay Lord".

I wondered what the tenants living in the apartments next to me thought a few months ago when I had what I call a loud emotional outburst. After weeks of searching for work and the mounds of bills continuing to pile up, fear and hopelessness set in. Why not move back home? Are you serious? When I left, let's just say it wasn't a happy "send off." One of my sisters had recently asked if I had found a job. When I replied "no", she said, "Well, you should have kept your a** at home!" So needless to say, things weren't going so well and the pressure was building. Like a whistling tea kettle, I spewed forth my frustrations and fears to my Heavenly Father.

"If the people in my hometown, my family, my former church leaders only knew... If they could see me now...the predicament I've gotten myself into, the dilemma I'm facing, they really would think I'm a "fanatic!" Who in their right mind leaves their home, their family, moves to a strange city with no job and no place to live, just because "God says so?!""

• **You said,** "To get out from among my kindred and go to a place I will show you!"

• **You said,** "You would never leave me nor forsake me!"

• **You said,** "Not to worry about what I would eat or drink or the clothing I would wear... for your heavenly Father knows you need all of these things!"

• **You said,** "The righteous shall never be forsaken; nor your seed begging for bread!"

- **You said,** *"Ask and it will be given to you; Seek and you will find; Knock and it will be opened to you!"* (Matthew 7:7)

"Well here I am! I am scared! I am a young woman all alone in a strange city! I have no job! I am here because you told me to come! What I am supposed to do here? What am I supposed to do about the car payment, the rent, school loans and utility bills? You know there's not enough money in my bank account to cover all of these!"

Finally my screaming, crying and pacing subsided. I sat on the sofa exhausted and probably looking like a total mess when I heard Him say, **"You forgot one thing."** "What?!" I asked, thinking I have no more energy to spend. "**Thank Me**," He said. **"Faith is not about seeing; it's about believing Me."** Suddenly, my crushed spirit was rejuvenated! My batteries had somehow been recharged! With a tear-stained face, my hands lifted, I ran through the apartment thanking and praising God! It was a done deal! I did not know the specifics, but I knew my heavenly Father was already taking care of things!

This new journey was not only stretching my faith and challenging my obedience, but it was also building my trust in God. I was starting to know Him more intimately. Before, I had only known Him as Savior, Creator of the universe, and my Heavenly Father. During the next months, He revealed more of Himself. I would come to know Him as Jehovah-Jireh, the Provider! There were no more hysterical meltdowns, but there were plenty of "I can't believe this is happening" days like:

• The unexplained checks arriving in the mail totaling the amount of my rent and car payment. (In utter disbelief, I made countless telephone calls to the companies that had issued the checks, only to be told the checks were valid and no mistakes had been made. Again before cashing them, I called and was given reassurance that there were no discrepancies. The checks were official.)

• A notification of a package to be picked up at the post office. The "package" was a box so large it barely fit into the backseat of my car. I struggled from the parking lot to the apartment wondering what could possibly be in this box that was 5 feet tall. *(Just for the record, I stand only 5 feet, 2 and ½ inches tall. And yes, Friend, when one is vertically challenged, a half of an inch is a "big" deal.)* My exhaustion gave way to curiosity as I anxiously opened the gigantic box shipped from an address in Everett, Washington. A note within the box contained the message, "The Lord laid it on my heart to do this. I hope these are the right size! Love, Monica". Every suit, each pair of slacks, shirts, sweaters, blouses, and jeans all fit like a glove. Each item was exactly my taste. It was as if God had blessed me with my very own "personal shopper".

When leaving for work, I discovered the bags of groceries left at my door early one morning. The items within the bags contained the exact items I was out of and the exact foods I usually eat. (I, being a very finicky eater, was surprised to see the food items were the brands I preferred.) No one had rung my doorbell; there had not been a knock at the door and no one left a note.

A surprise call came from Ms. Lewis who lived in Michigan and called to inform me to be on the lookout for a $100 check she was placing in the mail. She wanted to bless me with a trip to the hair salon. I thanked her and after hanging up the phone, I resorted to my "needing to know" ways. Why is Ms. Lewis doing this? It's not my birthday; I asked partly in disbelief and partly trying to understand.

"She has the same Father as you do", the Holy Spirit answered.

Pieces of the puzzle were now starting to fit together. Although the waters were deep and swirling, I began to realize I was not alone. *He* was providing for my every need, even those I hadn't yet asked for. A smile came across my face when I read Psalm 8:4: *"What is man that you are mindful of him, and the son of man that you visit him?"*

A wave of relief washed over me as I pondered the meaning of this verse. It was comforting to know God was "mindful of me," and somehow I knew I could completely trust Him to handle any storms that arose in my life.

Dear friend,

Are you, like me, beginning to understand God has a purpose for everything He does? I am curious as to what He has planned at the hair salon. Care to join me?

Day of Beauty

"So what brought you to this city?" the owner of the salon asked.

As I recounted the "happenings" that resulted in my moving to Sparta, the salon owner was genuinely interested and wanted to hear more. It just so happened she had an opening later that day. "Thank you, Lord". It was such a treat to be pampered. The recent weeks had been so stressful and trying. It was as if I had been treading water to stay afloat—no rescue boat, no search party in sight, just a small fish in deep waters.

The hairstylists were accommodating and friendly, and the shop was warm and inviting, serving only a few clients that day. My attention was drawn to a little boy who looked to be two-years-old. He quietly sat watching cartoons while his mom's hair was being styled. Such a well-behaved and contented child, I thought. Then my mind drifted to the goodness of God and my appreciation for this much needed pampering. My thoughts were interrupted as a lady in the shop suddenly cried out. "What's wrong?" I asked,

62

having noticed one of the stylists holding the little boy in her arms. It appeared he was having a seizure, for his lips had turned blue and his eyes were rolled upward.

Someone dialed 911 and in the middle of the chaos, I heard the familiar voice of the Holy Spirit say **"Do you see this?"** My hands began to tingle and became noticeably warmer. It was the strangest thing, yet somehow, I knew I was being led into these new waters to help the little boy. I placed my hands on the child and began to pray. There was no change evident in the boy's condition. He remained limp in the stylist's arms. I looked toward heaven and asked "What else Lord?" **"You forgot one thing,** He said, **thank me."**

"Now faith is the substance of things hoped for, the evidence of things not seen." (Hebrews 11:1)

The salon then became a house of praise as I unashamedly lifted my voice, praising and thanking God for His healing power. In the midst of giving God praise, the boy came out of the seizure! The paramedics arrived, examined the boy, and gave us an exasperated look as if we, "silly women", had wasted their time. The boy appeared to be okay, but as a precautionary measure he was taken to the hospital for further examination. The medical team at the hospital concluded the boy was fine and released him into the care of his mother.

The stylist who had been holding the boy looked at me with tears in her eyes and said, "I heard you pray and I know what happened."

"Who do you believe 'touched' this boy?", I asked her.

She responded "Jesus!"

"Amen, He certainly did! Praise the Lord."

Dear Friend,

A lesson I have learned and am still learning is, these waters are never still. For once you step out into these waters, your life will never be the same. Gone are the days of my having a personal agenda, doing things my way, and thinking I have all of the answers. Yes, my friend, within these ever moving waters, God will take what seems to be an ordinary day and turn it into an extraordinary adventure. One just never knows quite what to expect!

Stay with me and you will see what I mean.

Teresa L. Colbert

A Country Welcome

Julie Ann, a struggling single mom, worked hard to provide for her son. She wanted him to have a better life than hers. Her dreams for him included college, a good job and a happy life. She, like me, was working two part-time jobs while waiting for permanent, full-time employment.

"You're not from Sparta, are you?" she asked. "No," I replied.

"Why did you decide to move here?"

Our fifteen-minute break was almost over, so I gave her the "condensed version", but agreed to meet in the parking lot after our shift ended to resume our conversation.

"So what do you have planned for the weekend?" Julie Ann asked. Before I could answer, Julie Ann excitedly told me about her church's annual homecoming celebration and how "she would love for me to come". Why not, I didn't have any other plans. "I will see you Sunday morning."

Could this be right? Did I take a wrong turn? Julie Ann's directions were simple: Turn right onto Church Street and drive 11 miles. Turn left at the traffic light. Cross over the railroad tracks. The church was on the right. Cars were lined along the graveled road leading to the small country church. Children were excitedly running and playing. Men dressed in jeans and plaid shirts were standing near the front entrance of the church greeting people as they entered. Older women wearing aprons and bonnets were busy arranging their food baskets under the covered pavilion. Somehow Julie Ann had failed to mention the words "old fashioned, country, church picnic on the grounds" when she issued the invitation. Feeling slightly "overdressed" in my designer suit and 3" inch heels and seriously wishing I had time to go home and change into something more casual, quickly gave way to another realization. **The designer's suit and 3" heels are not the only things different about you.** I smiled, said hello, and felt the curious eyes follow me as I walked by.

Julie Ann waved, wiped perspiration from her brow, and scurried from the canopy to meet me. I smiled as Julie Ann introduced me to her son and others as they entered the small sanctuary. Within a matter of minutes, there was a steady stream of people filing in. Julie Ann's help was needed at the pavilion, so I selected a seat at the end of a pew by an open window. Yes, this was indeed homecoming. Relatives and friends were busy shaking hands and giving hugs. A family of seven shared a pew with me. As I continued to look around, I noticed there was no air conditioning and, once again, found myself wishing I had worn something a little more casual!

Thoughts of my discomfort soon subsided when I suddenly became aware of the reason for my being there. It was not to merely visit and attend a worship service. I was there on an assignment! **"Do you see her? Turn around. She is seated on the back row."** Although there were several young ladies seated on the back pew, somehow I knew which one *HE* was referring to. She had dark brown hair and was seated on the far end of the row. I guessed her age to be maybe twenty-years-old. The morning worship service was due to start soon, but apparently *HE* had a different idea of how today's service would be conducted.

However, Jesus was known to occasionally interrupt religious meetings. I recalled reading about a particular time during one such service when *His* attention was turned to a woman whose need was greater than another "Sunday-go-to-meeting service.

"Now He was teaching in one of the synagogues on the Sabbath. And, behold, there was a woman who had a spirit of infirmity eighteen years, and was bent over and could in no way raise herself up. But when Jesus saw her, He called her to him, and said to her, "Woman, you are loosed from your infirmity." And He laid his hands on her: and immediately she was made straight, and glorified God." (Luke 13: 10-13)

"Excuse me." I carefully crossed over the family of seven, made my way down the narrow aisle and politely maneuvered onto the back pew and sat next to *her*. As one might expect, she was somewhat surprised at my infringement. And she wasn't the only one! Squeezing onto a cramped pew and interrupting an ongoing conversation was totally uncharacteristic of me! But, gradually, I was beginning to understand none of the unusual occurrences "about me."

"Hi. My name is Ry'ah. I am not sure why, but the Lord sent me to talk to you. He wants you to know how much He loves you and He has a plan for your life." The girl said nothing as the tears rolled down her face. Then all of a sudden, she hugged me, took my hand and together we ran to the altar. On our knees, I prayed as the young woman sobbed, broken and contrite before the Lord. Across the sanctuary, others erupted in praise and thanksgiving. Women gathered around to embrace the young woman and I returned to my seat, carefully crossing over the family of seven again. My heart swelled as I contemplated the never-ending love of God. The preacher stood in amazement, thanking God for what had just occurred, describing it as a miracle. Due to excessive drug abuse and riotous living, Sarah, the young lady, had been estranged from her family for a very long time. The church had been faithfully praying for her for many years and today she had returned to God and to her family. The preacher then asked me to stand, introduce myself and welcomed any words I'd like to share. I spoke briefly giving all the praise and glory to God. I would have said more, but my "cup was running over".

"Ain't that just like God?" the preacher said. He sent this young lady all the way from the mountains of North Carolina to guide this prodigal daughter home. Hallelujah!"

Dear Friend,

I never anticipated along this journey, there would be periods of loneliness. Oh sure the GUIDE is here with me, but sometimes He is quiet ...actually, at times, I find Him to be too quiet. I'm not sure what He does during those times. Maybe He is consulting with His Father or tending to others' requests or maybe He is resting. I've read He is known to have some "quiet time" occasionally.

"Immediately Jesus made His disciples get into the boat and go before Him to the other side, while He sent the multitudes away. And when He had sent the multitudes away, He went up on the mountain by Himself to pray. Now when evening came, He was alone there." (Matthew 14:22-23)

"Now in the morning, having risen a long while before daylight, He went out and *departed to a solitary place; and there He prayed."* (Mark 1:35)

"...In those days that He went out to the mountain to pray, and continued all night in prayer to God." (Luke 6:12)

You know, come to think of it, I may find Him in my living room. There's a chair by the window which has become our special place. And it's there I sit for hours, never tiring of hearing His still small voice. He's fascinating company. Ask Mary, she'll agree with me.

"Now it happened as they went that He entered a certain village; and a certain woman named Martha welcomed Him into her house. And she had a sister called Mary, who also sat at Jesus' feet and heard His word." (Luke 10:38, 39)

He's a great listener and surprisingly, He is easy to talk to. What do we talk about? Anything... Everything...

Teresa L. Colbert

Say What and Do What?

76

Oh how I longed for a place to gather with other believers and worship. So finding a church home became a priority. But things were different here so very different. There were many Sunday mornings in which I awakened early, dressed and prepared to go in search of finding a "good church", only to be redirected by the Holy Spirit. Imagine my surprise when *He* informed me I **would not be attending church today. I was to go by the hospital instead.** None of this made any sense to me. I needed to be in church, I persisted. I needed to find a good church. I could go to the hospital after church, but I needed ...

Apparently, I <u>needed</u> a lesson, so the TEACHER commenced to teach: "**Ry'ah, what is a church?**" "It's a body of baptized believers." (I knew this answer, learned it in Sunday school.) "**Yes, but you tend to view the church as a building with a steeple. There are people who will never come to the 'building with a steeple'.**

Many have been wounded in the building. Some feel so unworthy. Others think they lack

the proper clothes. Some may not be physically able to come to a building.

I need someone who will go to them. Whom shall I send? Will you go for us?"

The Teacher had taught. The lesson had been given. What would be my answer? "Yes, Lord. I'll go". But true to my nature I had lots of questions, which was okay because *HE* had the answers!

The city of Sparta had several hospitals. Which one? I don't know anyone in the hospital, so why am I going to the hospital? Who am I supposed to be going to see at the hospital? What am I to do when I get there, what floor? What room number?

I was only given one answer, the name of the hospital. After I arrived there and parked the car, I was given the floor and room numbers and nothing more, no names, no further instructions. So I presumed and accepted the very real possibility that whenever I walked into these "rooms", people would think me to be a religious nut, call security and have me escorted from the premises. Maybe that's why God's word tells us

78

"...And lean not on your own understanding" (Proverbs 3:5)

Surprisingly the patients and visiting family members alike were found to be receptive and responsive as I was led by the Holy Spirit to anoint them with oil and pray. *"And the prayer of faith will save the sick, and the Lord will raise him up. And if he has committed sins, he will be forgiven."* (James 5:15) I witnessed miracle after miracle as God touched lives, healed patients and "confounded the wise".

For those who would think me strange or fanatical, I offer you my Father's perspective: "Peculiar."

*"But ye are a chosen generation, a royal priesthood, a holy nation, a **peculiar people**; that ye should shew forth the praises of him who hath called you out of darkness into his marvelous light."* (1 Peter 2:9, KJV)

Our heavenly Father is still seeking and asking. Do you hear him? Listen.

"Also I heard the voice of the Lord, saying: "Whom shall I send, and who will go for us?"...
(Isaiah 6:8, KJV)

What will be your answer? Are you willing? If your answer is "Yes," I congratulate you my friend. Welcome to the journey beyond shallow waters. These deeper waters are overwhelming and yet, marvelous at the same time. Sometimes, though, they can be very, very lonely. Yeah sure, you'll frequently meet others who have answered the call to venture out here, but sadly many return to the familiar shallow waters. They find the cost is too great, the assignments too challenging, the discipline too demanding and the sacrifice unrewarding. And while I may experience periods of loneliness, I have no desire to turn back. My steps are ordered by the Lord, and I will continue to follow Him into the deep.

My Friend, I hope you aren't ready to turn back. It's an awesome journey, and we've just begun! There is yet more territory to cover, more adventure to come, more assignments to complete. Stay with me. It's nice having you along sharing this extraordinary journey.

"Some people enter our lives and leave
almost instantly. Others stay, and forge
such an impression on our heart and soul,
we are changed forever."

Author unknown

Hanging Out With Ma

How could I say "no" to her? Ma, as she was affectionately called, had opened her home and her heart to include me and now she was inviting me into her inner circle and social gatherings. The holidays would soon be approaching. Her missionary circle was busy planning its Christmas party and Ma would like for me to be her guest. Oh my goodness! These women are 30 years my senior. Will I be the only young woman at their party? Probably! But if Ma is there, this will be a party you will not want to miss!

Dear friend,

I am not sure my words can do Ma justice, but I'll make an honorable attempt to portray her and hopefully capture the essence of this amazing lady who has greatly enriched my life.

Interested in meeting her? Of course, you may find you have already crossed paths with Ma... in fact you may have chatted with her in a waiting room...sat next to her on a flight, shook hands with her at a convention, bumped into her at the train station, stood in line with her in the grocery store, or it is very likely you may have met her at your family reunion! Ma seems to know somebody in every state of the Union. So, don't be the least surprised if she knows your grandmother, cousins, aunts, pastor or your neighbor! Yeah, you might say this little lady "gets around". Oh, and another thing about Ma, what you see is what you get... and you're in for a treat 'cause Ma is a bundle of love.

Kari and I had been fervently working on an important project that was due within a few days. In order to meet the deadline, we started work early, skipped breaks and ate lunch at our desks.

We purposefully tuned out the occasional distractions of telephones ringing, the humming of the printer, and the never-ending pages blaring over the intercom system. We had made great strides and were on target to complete the project before noon on Friday. As an incentive, Peter, our supervisor, had promised to take us out for lunch and give us the afternoon off. For a free lunch and a Friday afternoon off, we were determined to get the job done!

About 10:15 a.m. all work came to a halt! No, it wasn't due to a power outage. No, we weren't called in to an important meeting. No, it wasn't one of those inconvenient fire drills. The interruption was MA! A petite, feisty, outspoken woman with a commanding presence entered the office and unquestionably shifted the atmosphere.

"Hey! How is everybody? What's going on? Nobody died, did they? It's too blamed quiet in here!" It's Ma, so work would have to wait.

"Now, Ms. Ruby," Peter begins in a chiding tone.

Dear Friend, I need to pause here and let you in on a pertinent piece of information. Ms. Ruby (Ma) is Peter's mother and things are about to get interesting.

Ma frowns at his chiding tone and proceeds to tell him "while he may be a supervisor telling other folks what to do...." you get the picture. Well, Peter got the point, returned to his desk and said nothing further. Ma visited with us for a few more minutes. Kari and I quietly asked if she thought Peter was upset with her, to which she replied, "If he lives long enough, he'll get over it, or he'll die mad. After all, he must remember I had him. I'm his Ma!"

If you ever need a weekend of fun-filled adventure, then I recommend hanging out with Ma. The only thing you need is lots of energy because she is constantly on the go! Ma had invited me to hang out with her over the weekend.

"Just us chicks," she said. We arrived at her house after work on a Friday evening. I assumed after working all week, Ma would probably put on house slippers, have dinner, settle in to watch "Wheel of Fortune" and then nod off. I soon found out that's not exactly what "hanging out" with Ma entails. No, it wasn't slippers Ma changed into, it was black leather! That's right, leather! Leather pants, leather jacket and a leather cap.

This "ball of energy" drives like one too! Although she is a good driver, please buckle-up, because you'll be in for the ride of your life! To the mall we went for Ma needed a new hat! We had a leisurely dinner, but Ma was surprised at how little I ate and compared it to "eating like a bird". We stopped in to visit a few of her friends whom she wanted me to meet and after hours of visiting, we arrived back at Ma's house. Still burning with lots of energy, we talked well into the night before retiring for bed.

Widowed at 24 years of age, Ma was left alone to raise four children. Countless hours I sat at her kitchen table enamored by the many years of accrued wisdom, belly laughed more than I ever have in my life, fought back tears for all of the heartache she experienced, and admired her deeply as she gave me a stroll down her "memory lane".

Ma was the eldest of ten children and learned to wash and cook at the age of nine. Her birth was the result of her mother having been sexually abused by a "white man." At times she was treated differently because she had "good hair" and light- colored skin. She treasured the precious one pair of nylons she had and hand washed them gingerly. Never on welfare, she sometimes worked two and three jobs to put food on the table. She made regrettable mistakes along the way, but did the best she could.

Then there is the hilarious story of the "red petticoat." *Sorry friend, but only Ma can tell this one!* If it had not been for the Lord, she wouldn't have made it!

Ma doesn't live in a house filled with fancy things, but her freezer is full of food: ready to be shared with the family who just lost their loved one, the neighbor who is sick and in bed, a single mother struggling to raise her children, the potluck dinners at church or anyone who just happens to stop in for a visit.

No, she does not live in a fancy house, but my friend if you are:

- lonely, you'll find a true friend at Ma's house.
- down and discouraged, you'll find kindness and encouragement at Ma's house.
- hungry, you'll find a home cooked meal at Ma's house.
- weary, you'll find rest and comfort at Ma's house.
- in need of lots of love, you'll find it at Ma's house.

Dear friend, earlier I stated I wasn't sure my words could do Ma justice, nor capture the essence of this amazing lady, but I read something that comes close:

"Love suffers long and is kind; love does not envy; love does not parade itself, is not puffed up; does not behave rudely, does not seek its own, is not provoked, thinks no evil." (1 Corinthians 13: 4-5)

Ma was my encourager; and oh how I needed encouraging during those times when I couldn't see the light at the end of the tunnel. Ma always had the right words to lift your spirit. "Turn it over to the Lord, baby. Just pray, and keep praying and everything is going to be all right. Just keep on trusting the Lord, you hear?" Then there were those unforgettable life nuggets she shared:

- "It's a poor frog who praises his own pond."
- "Don't worry, if they live long enough, they'll get over it, or they'll die mad."
- "Just keep living baby, just keep living."
- "Be careful not to burn bridges. They may be the same planks you'll need to cross back over one day."

Oops! Ma will be here any minute. I hope you are coming to the party with us. But we must hurry, we can't keep Ma waiting.

Guess Who's Coming to Dinner?

A sophisticated, wintry mix of silver and white decorations filled the garden room glittering within the confines of good taste. White sprayed tree branches and tiny Italian lights created a picture-perfect ambiance as did the white pillar candles with silver ribbon going down the center of the table. Yes, indeed. It was beginning to look a lot like Christmas!

Every table was filled and it was apparent business was thriving. The restaurant seemed to be a popular venue during the holiday season as numerous parties were underway on this spectacular evening. Tasty food, lots of laughter, and fun made for a delightful evening. Ma was in rare form, making witty comments and "being the life of the party".

I'm really glad I came and I'm actually having a good time even though I am "partying" with people 30 years older than me.

The small talk, laughter, and enjoyable evening were interrupted by a commotion across the room. One of the ladies within our party had collapsed onto the floor. Others were attending to her and seemed to have things under control. "It's good they know CPR," I thought. "I certainly don't!" I wasn't aware there was a *Special Guest* present at this gathering until I heard His voice say to me, "**Do you see this**?", referring to the incident of the woman lying on the floor. Then as if echoing His words, Ma said, "Do you see this? Please go over and see if you can help Ms. Whitfield." I realize that I am not just attending a dinner party, but I am being ushered into deeper waters.

I waded through the large crowd that had gathered around the woman, and requested all to give me room. These were not friendly waters. Intimidating waves surfaced through the stern faces and belligerent voices. But with the same authority of HIM who spoke to the winds and waves and they obeyed His voice, I spoke to the threatening obstinate forces to move! All stood back and I saw Ms. Whitfield lying on the floor.

I knelt beside her and took her hand. "Can you hear me?" I asked. She nodded yes. "What is your name?" I asked. She spoke her name faintly. "My name is Ry'ah," I told her. "Tell me how you're feeling?"

"I can hear you, but I can't see you. My heart is beating so fast," she said.

"Do you know Jesus?" I asked. "Yes," she said.

"Well, do you mind if I talk to Him about you for a few minutes?"

"Okay," she said.

With the power, guidance, and anointing of the Holy Spirit, I prayed for Ms. Whitfield. Sometime during the prayer, the paramedics had arrived and after commencing with "amen", I opened my eyes to find them kneeling beside her. They were asking questions as they examined her eyes.

"I was blind, but now I see," she told them. They checked her heart with a stethoscope and she said, "My heart has been regulated!" I noticed her voice was getting stronger and growing with

96

excitement. The paramedics found nothing to be wrong with her.

"Tell them who touched you and what happened," I encouraged her.

"Jesus, Jesus!" she shouted. The restaurant became a sanctuary and the dinner party became a jubilee as I praised the Lord for His goodness! Ms. Whitfield was taken to the hospital for further observation and was released the next morning with a "clean bill of health"!

"And the prayer of faith will save the sick, and the Lord will raise him up. And if he has committed sins, he will be forgiven." (James 5:15) What a mighty God we, serve!

Dear Friend,

The journey beyond shallow waters experience is a life of complete surrendering unto the Lord. Each day out here in these deeper waters is life-changing. I never know what to expect, but I am to live in a state of expectancy. I'm learning to "look for Him"; and often times, I find Him beyond the four walls of the church building, in the most unconventional places. So don't be surprised if you "happen" upon Him mingling at your dinner party!

"God, send me anywhere, only go with me.
Lay any burden on me, only sustain me.

And sever any tie in my heart, except the tie
that binds my heart to yours."

David Livingstone

Teresa L. Colbert

"Please Say, You'll Come"

Some invitations are nothing more than small pleas that tug on your heartstrings. Heartstrings, we all have them. Fathers' heartstrings are pulled by their little girls. Pet owners' heart strings are pulled by brown-eyed puppies; and grandparents' heartstrings are pulled by their adorable grandchildren. Before your lips can form a refusal, your heart is overridden with an affirmative. I felt my heartstrings being tugged as Angela desperately and tearfully pleaded, "Maybe you can talk to him? Please. He may listen to you. Please, say you'll come!"

A recent phone conversation with her brother had left Angela with an unsettling feeling; one she couldn't seem to shake. He had talked of not having a reason to live and she worried he might try to harm himself. Her attempts to encourage him, promises to visit soon and frequent letters had not been effective. She described him as being in a state of hopelessness, and herself as feeling helpless. I wasn't quite sure as to why Angela was asking me for help. I didn't know her brother and I had only known Angela for a few months. If he were indeed depressed as she surmised, then surely her minister, another family member, or perhaps his counselor would be better suited to talk to him. Besides, what made her think he would listen to anything I, a total stranger, would say? But there was something about her desperate pleading and love for her brother that tugged on my heartstrings. I wonder if this was the same type of pleading that moved Jesus' heartstrings when Jairus petitioned Him for help.

"And behold, one of the rulers of the synagogue came, Jairus by name. And when he saw Him, he fell at His feet and begged Him earnestly, saying, "My little daughter lies at the point of death. Come and lay Your hands on her, that she may be healed, and she will live." So Jesus went with him, and a great multitude followed Him and thronged Him." (Mark 5:22-24a)

"Yes, I'll go," I agreed.

Once again I find myself questioning God, "What am I doing here?" Then I remember the sincere prayer in which I commit to the Lord, "I will go wherever you want; any door you open, I'll go through." I really meant those words—but I had no idea these words would lead me through barbed wire fences, guard dogs and prison doors. "O Lord, what do I do, what do I say?"

I wonder what crime he has committed. My heart is beating so fast and I jump as the prison doors slam shut behind me. Walking quietly but frantically toward the Visitor's Center, I am not sure of what type of man I will encounter. Angela had not revealed much about her brother, only that he was in trouble and needed someone to talk to. "Lord, what if this man I am about to meet is a murderer or a rapist?" The answer... **Then he is a qualified candidate for salvation, for in order to be saved, one must be lost".**

Remembering the safety I'd once known from within the small, close-knit mountain community, I marvel as this journey continues into uncertain, sometimes turbulent, dark, fearful, deep waters. Though questions continue to surface and fear swells around me, I forge ahead all the while certain the Master of the deep is bidding me, leading me, and maneuvering me through these uncharted waters.

> *"I will bring the blind by a way they did not know; I will lead them in paths they have not known. I will make darkness light before them, and crooked places straight. These things I will do for them, and not forsake them."* (Isaiah 42:16)

I cautiously entered the Visitor's center, taking deep breaths and occasionally pinching myself and hoping this was a dream I would soon awaken from. To try and calm my nerves, I scanned the non-descript room, taking inventory which took all of about 20 seconds: fifteen cafeteria style tables with attached chairs and three vending machines. Family members and friends waited anxiously as buzzers sounded from time to time indicating prisoners were entering the room. I waited unobtrusively and quietly at a corner table, observing as men with somber expressions, dressed in orange jumpsuits emerged. Like sun rays piercing a dark sky, melancholy faces ignited with smiles at the sound of children gleefully shouting, "Daddy, Daddy," and loved ones embracing them. Oddly, only minutes before, this room had been unnervingly quiet, but now was buzzing with chatter and robust laughter. The buzzer sounded again, the door opened and in walked another prisoner. His eyes curiously perused the room, and as if by process of elimination, he walked towards the table where I was sitting. Admittedly, I was somewhat relieved when his countenance seemed to portray a non-threatening pose. "Hello. My name is Ry'ah." He paused, looked around the room once more and then reservedly took a seat.

The young man, Jonathan I learned, had obviously made some bad choices which had eventually led him to prison. Dropping out of school, possession of stolen goods, violating probation and the latest drug bust were listed on his rap sheet. A tiny jail cell with cold concrete floors would be his home for many years, but as I talked with him, I soon realized he had been imprisoned long before he came to the penitentiary.

Jonathan's childhood innocence was apprehended the day he came home from school and found his mother lying on the floor, dead from a self-inflicted gunshot wound. She left without saying goodbye...she left without answering, why Mama? She left an eight-year-old whose innocence was now locked away.

Bedtime stories and "pleasant dreams" were replaced by horrific nightmares and startling screams. Skinned knees accompanied by a tear-streaked face longed for Mama's kisses "to make it better." He exited the school bus in the afternoon, longing to see his mother's smiling face. He now rode his bike past the "house" that would never again be his home.

The haunting memory, unexplained questions, and tragic loss of the only "real" love he had ever known, left Jonathan emotionally imprisoned, sinking deeper into hopelessness. And even now as I sit with him, he still struggles to be free of those dark, murky waters: free from despair, free from the pain, free from guilt and free from the torment.

Abruptly the conversation changed course. Apparently the discussion was too intense... I had plunged too deep. Jonathan seemed to prefer staying above the surface by making jokes and flirtatious comments. However, I chose not to tread in those shallow waters and continued to dive deeper surveying the wreckage that held him captive. Then the accusatory questions started, "Who are you really? Why did you come? I'm a stranger to you. What's in it for you?" He assured me he was familiar with the stale water of religion. He had attended church services a few times and wondered which "pool" I swam in: Baptist, Catholic, Church of God, Jehovah Witness, Methodist, Muslim, Mormon, or another religion? He had sat by the side of each of these religious pools, only dangling his feet, but never desiring to jump in.... they were too cold and uninviting.

I waited for the "Lifeguard's" leading before tossing Jonathan the "Life-Preserver". "I came because I love Jesus and I made Him a promise.... I would go wherever He leads me and share Him with anyone who needs Him." No matter what has happened in your life that's led you here, you can be free behind these prison walls. *"Therefore if the Son makes you free, you shall be free indeed."* (John 8:36). I shared how Jesus had died for him and for me, His plan of salvation, and that He desired a relationship with Jonathan. Jesus wanted to teach him how to walk and live this Christian life.

The Holy Spirit began to soften Jonathan's heart and the Word of God penetrated the once hardened shell. Tears welled up in his eyes, his voice filled with emotion as he expressed how no one had ever taken the time to explain these things to him. Time passed quickly and visiting hours were drawing to a close. Jonathan bowed his head as I began to talk to Jesus about this young man and to thank *Him* for allowing our paths to cross, for giving us this opportunity to talk and how our lives would never be the same. Jonathan prayed to receive Christ, smiled and took my hand and thanked me for coming. He tried to convey what he was feeling at that moment. "I've never felt quite like this before...for the first time in my life, I feel...I feel... FREE!"

Dear friend,

Do you know of anyone who's:

- *hurting and in despair?*
- *in need of God's love and mercy?*
- *hungry or sick or in prison?*
- *in turmoil and searching for peace?*
- *desperately needing to hear from the Christ in you?*

If so, I pray you will listen closely. Then maybe you will feel the tug of your heartstrings and respond to their heartfelt plea, "Please say you'll come." I guarantee it's an invitation you will not want to pass up!

Matthew 25:36 & 40: *"...I was in prison and you came to me...Assuredly I say to you, in as much as you did it to one of the least of these, my brethren, you did it to me."*

Teresa L. Colbert

"Broken Things Can Become Blessed Things

If

You Let GOD Do the Mending"

Unknown

Go Get
Your Brother

Ah....There's nothing quite like the smell of steaks and hamburgers sizzling on the grill! The tantalizing aromas wafted into the house only to heighten our mouthwatering anticipation. Our guests had arrived early, so we were busy chatting, preparing the sides and enjoying the fun and fellowship. It was an absolutely picture-perfect evening—soft music playing in the background, a spectacular sunset and scrumptious food soon to be served. Oops, excuse me, the phone is ringing...

"Hello." The fury! The anguish! The terror! The rage that followed my "hello" sent my heart pounding, my mind racing and my lips stammering. Could *"hell hath no fury like a woman scorned"* be playing out before my eyes?" Lord, please help me! Help me help her. Throw me a life preserver...this water is too deep......the torrents are too treacherous.....two lives are in danger of drowning.......S.O.S. Mayday! Mayday!

Dinner would have to wait! The perfect evening had been sabotaged by a sadistic intruder. The enemy had launched a vicious attack

114

on the holy institution of marriage and prayer warriors were needed to do battle against the forces of hell. Justin and Elaine were in for the fight of their lives and had been deceived into thinking this one devastating display would destroy their thirty-plus years of marriage. These empty nesters were growing so faithfully in their walk with God. Their joys included traveling, dining out, babysitting the grandchildren and spending quiet evenings together. No one saw it coming, but that's exactly how Satan operates, *walking "...about like a roaring lion, seeking whom he may devour."* (1 Peter 5:8) Yes, this trap was strategically set, "a fowler's snare". "2 for 1" or so the enemy thought, but the devil is a liar!

Dear Friend,

Have you ever lived in a small community where everyone knows each other by their first names and people within the community wave to one another as they pass by? Kids gather to play at the end of the street and all goes well until a nose bleed occurs or a knee is scraped or the occasional "cat fight" erupts.

Yes and then there are those "exceptional neighbors" who will forever be embedded in your memory: Catherine and Doug, the high school sweethearts who married and now have two sets of twins. They live next door to Ms. Lawson, a widow, who is constantly shooing the kids off of her meticulously manicured lawn. Then there's Gloria who talks nonstop about her precious, talented, adorable, handsome, captain of the football team son whom others seem to describe as a smart-mouthed brat! The new couple who moved here from Ohio, Steve and Marlene Edwards, bought the Johnson place and tend to keep to themselves. Not even Ms. Berkley, the informed, community "busybody", could muster up any juicy news regarding them.

In this small community, a newspaper isn't necessary for the local current events. News is primarily shared at the neighbor's fence, or while lingering after the Wednesday night church meeting, or at a baby shower or one of those infamous phone calls beginning with, "Have you heard?" What I find to be very interesting and yet disturbing about this method of communication is, oftentimes, most of what is shared is fabricated. In the absence of information, people tend to fill in the blanks. The juicier the tale, the faster it spreads and sadly, the more damage is done. So was the case involving Justin and Elaine.

News of this particular scandal rapidly filtered through the small community and became the hot topic for weeks on end: "*A marriage on the rocks, husband & wife separate.*" Telephones were buzzing; people took time out of their mundane schedules "to visit". No one rushed home for Sunday dinner, but lingered hoping to catch any further news. As you may suspect, neighbors, extended family members, and sadly, members of the local church were excitedly *talking about* Justin

118

and Elaine but no one was *talking to* them. No words of comfort... no words of hope, no Godly counsel, only whispers of mean, cruel gossip and the occasional, "If it were me, I'd divorce him," advice. All the while, the *"Accuser of the brethren"* continued his onslaught of scheming and lying. His apparent intention was for this marriage to drown in the bitter waters of divorce. His mission was to destroy their lives. But Jesus, who "...*came that they might have life and have it more abundantly"* (John 10:10), had another plan for this marriage! He dispatched a search and rescue team of praying Christians to administer His love to this distraught couple.

Immediately, the prayer team began to assemble on the front lines of this battle, wielding the Word of God.

"Finally my brethren, be strong in the Lord and in the power of His might. Put on the whole armor of God that you may be able to stand against the wiles of the devil. For we do not wrestle against flesh and blood but principalities, against powers, against the rulers of the darkness of this age,

against spiritual hosts of wickedness in the heavenly places." (Ephesians 6: 10-12)

"For the weapons of our warfare are not carnal, but mighty in God for pulling down strongholds, casting down arguments and every high thing that exalts itself against the knowledge of God, bringing every thought into captivity to the obedience of Christ." (2 Corinthians 10: 4, 5)

Over the course of the next several months, continuous streams of prayer, waves of encouragement, and strong currents of God's word flowed into the lives of Justin and Elaine.

Having awakened from a disturbing dream one night in which I saw a gun pointed at Justin's head, the Holy Spirit impressed upon me to go into intercessory prayer for Justin. The enemy was planning to take his life. The next morning, I received further instruction from the Lord, "**Go get your Brother**." I called the prayer team members who were ready and willing to make the four-hour trip to restore our brother.

120

Like a volcano spewing forth hot lava, Elaine's deep-seated bitterness, anger and resentment erupted as she detailed the painful events that occurred over the past months. Although Justin had hurt her deeply, admittedly, she still loved him. She worried about him and she missed him, but, what about her feelings? After all she had been the one made to look like a fool! She would never allow Justin to hurt her ever again! She would never trust him again! Tears rolled as she struggled with the shock of betrayal and the ongoing turmoil within. Elaine was in great need. She needed encouragement. She needed answers. She needed hope. I watched in awe as each member of the prayer team opened God's word and shared the truth in love with their hurting sister. Marion, who had experienced both betrayal and divorce after twenty-five years of marriage, shared about her decision to forgive and live in peace, rather than being overcome with bitterness. She then read 1 Corinthians 13: 4-7:

"Love suffers long and is kind; love does not envy; love does not parade itself, is not puffed up;

does not behave rudely, does not seek its own, is not provoked, thinks no evil; does not rejoice in iniquity, but rejoices in the truth; bears all things, believes all things, hopes all things, endures all things."

Within a few hours, Elaine had chosen forgiveness over bitterness. She was willing to trust God to give her *"...beauty for ashes."* (Isaiah 61:3)

Justin was now residing in a nearby town. The incredulous look on his face when the prayer team and Elaine arrived indicated we were the last people he had expected to see. The ordeal of the past months had obviously taken its toll on Justin. The sadness in his eyes... the weight loss... his haggard appearance and the smell of alcohol on his breath were evident. But a closer look revealed he was happy and quite relieved to see us, although somewhat embarrassed about the circumstances that led to this visit. Justin was known to be a gracious host, and today was no different as he invited us into his home. We embraced our estranged brother with love and were genuinely happy to see him. However, since this was not a social call and timing was of the essence, we needed to do what we had been "sent to do".

I began to share with Justin the reason for our visit. We had been earnestly praying for him. We had not come here today to judge him. Yes, we were aware of the "specifics". He had been snared by a ploy of the enemy. God had seen all, He knew all and God wanted to restore him. Most importantly, *He* still loved Justin and had a plan for his life.

Justin was noticeably struggling to stay alert. He admitted to drinking a few beers earlier that day. As the team began to pray quietly, the Holy Spirit revealed the enemy was present and was using the effects of the alcohol to distract Justin. Being led by the Spirit, I prayed and recalled Jesus' first miracle ... *turning water into wine* (John 2: 1-11) and then petitioned Him to perform a miracle by turning the alcohol inside Justin into water. Justin needed to hear the word of God.

"So then faith comes by hearing, and hearing by the word of God." (Romans 10:17)

In a matter of moments, Justin sat upright, his eyes were clear, his mind alert! God's word was opened and ministered to Justin.

1 John 1:9: *"If we confess our sins, He is faithful and just to forgive us our sins and to cleanse us from all unrighteousness."*

Galatians 6:1: *"Brethren, if a brother is overtaken in any trespass, you who are spiritual restore such a one in a spirit of gentleness, considering yourself lest you also be tempted."*

John 8:7: *"...He that is without sin among you, let him first cast a stone..."*

James 5: 19, 20: *"Brethren, if anyone among you wanders from the truth and someone turns him back, let him know that he who turns a sinner from the error of his way will save a soul from death and cover a multitude of sins."*

We witnessed further miracles as Justin was broken and humbled before God and his wife. He confessed and repented of his sin, poured out the case of beer that was in his refrigerator, pledged his love and devotion to his wife, and rededicated his life to God!

Though Elaine loved Justin and was witnessing these acts of obedience, she still doubted. Had their marriage reached the point of no return? Would he, could he keep his promises? She could forgive him, but could she trust him?

The fact remained Justin was fallible (just as we all are). He did not have the power to sustain himself (neither do we). Elaine then realized it was not Justin whom she needed to put her faith in, but God.

"And He said to me, "My grace is sufficient for you, for My strength is made perfect in weakness..." (2 Corinthians 12:9)

We watched as the love of God continued to wash over Justin and Elaine as they tearfully rushed into each other's arms.

It had been a long day, an exhausting day, but a glorious day. Tired in body, but elated in spirit, we prepared for the four-hour trek ahead of us and Justin and Elaine prepared to "go home together".

That has a nice sound to it. Doesn't it? Shall we end this one with, "and they lived happily ever after?" I'll admit I am partial to happy endings.

Ah, but not so fast. There was one piece of unfinished business....

What about the disturbing dream regarding an attempt on Justin's life?

As I shared the dream, his eyes widened in amazement and fear seemed to grip him like a boa constrictor squeezing its prey. Justin confirmed the dream was true. He hadn't told anyone. So how did I know? How could I know? Joey, a guy whom he had once regarded as his friend, recently put a gun to Justin's head and threatened to kill him. Joey, apparently in a drunken state and a fit of rage, was causing a disturbance. In an effort to try and calm him, Joey's rage escalated. Justin swallowed hard and shook his head in disbelief as the words "I thought he was my friend," fell from his lips.

We prayed with Justin and affirmed the Word of God over him.

Isaiah 54:17: *"No weapon formed against you shall prosper, and every tongue that rises against you in judgment you shall condemn..."*

2 Timothy 1:7: *"For God has not given us a spirit of fear, but of power and of love and of a sound mind."*

After months of being tossed about and tattered in a raging sea of despair and hopelessness, Justin and Elaine were guided to safe harbor.

The winds of hostility have ceased. The tidal waves of condemnation have long subsided, the billowing gossip now hushed, and their marriage now anchored in Christ.

Yes even today, JESUS *STILL SPEAKS TO THE WINDS AND WAVES AND THEY OBEY HIM!* (Matthew 8:27)

"... I have come into deep waters where the
floods overflow me."

Psalm 69:2

Teresa L. Colbert

Help Me!
I'm Drowning!

One of my favorite things to do is stroll along the beach at sunrise. There is something riveting about seeing the sun appear over the horizon and hearing the roar of the ocean.

Come. Walk with me. Take your shoes off, experience the feeling of the ripples and waves breaking into foam and swirling around your feet as we walk along the water's edge. Breathe in the invigorating saltwater air; feel the cool gentle breeze pressing ever so slightly against your back. I could stand for hours upon end gazing, oftentimes becoming mesmerized by the splendid view of the ocean that stretches far into the distance. Ah yes, this captivating place where:

• the water ends and the sky begins.

• your eye level and the vanishing point become inseparable.

• the sky and the earth appear to merge into one sea of blue.

131

Many times I'll catch glimpses of colorful sailboats in the distance, playful dolphins engaging in spectacular aerial presentations, and flocks of seagulls flying overhead. While I love taking in these panoramic, ocean views and breathing the invigorating ocean air, admittedly, there is no personal desire to venture into the depths of these vast waters. You see, swimming is not my forte. Therefore, snorkeling, deep sea diving and parasailing are better left to those thrill-seekers. (Any occasional exploring or close contact I may encounter with aquatic life most likely occurs at a large, state of the art aquarium.) However, there are many things I find fascinating about the ocean, among them being:

• About 70% of our planet is covered with water.

• Everything about the ocean is immense — it has the tallest mountains in the world and the deepest valleys.

• Most scientists think life began in the ocean over 3 billion years ago.

- Over 1 million known species of plants and animals live there, and scientists say there may be as many as 9 million species we haven't discovered yet.

While walking along with waves splashing against my ankles, I recall those awe-inspiring scriptures:

"In the beginning God created the heavens and the earth. The earth was without form, and void; and darkness was on the face of the deep. And the Spirit of God was hovering over the face of the waters." (Genesis 1:1, 2)

"Or who shut in the sea with doors, When it burst forth and issued from the womb; When I made the clouds its garment, And thick darkness its swaddling band; When I fixed My limit for it, And set bars and doors; When I said, 'This far you may come, but no farther,

And here your proud waves must stop!"
(Job 38:8-11)

And while the waves are inclined to be both alluring and welcoming, one should never underestimate the underlying force of the mighty deep. Its commanding presence is deserving of respectful attention. For within moments, strong swimmers and experienced surfers have been caught unaware and swept away by its abrupt rip currents while onlookers helplessly stood by.

The young woman found herself the victim of the unsuspecting rip currents of sin. The more she struggled against it, the deeper it seemed to pull her under. Preoccupied with their own interests, no one saw her struggle nor heard her inward cry, "Help me, I'm drowning!" Now she was in danger of being swept away.

Her blue eyes filled with tears and with trembling lips she confessed her secret to me. The secret is true. I could tell by the pleading look in Lori's eyes that seemed to say, "Please accept me; please help me; please understand ...please!" Oh my goodness! Stop! Too much information!

Why does she feel the need to share her secret with me? Why me? Shouldn't she be confiding in someone else, her pastor, or maybe better yet, a therapist? There is only one Counselor whom I know and can recommend. His name is Jesus! *"He is a very present help in trouble."* (Psalm 46:1) The truth and freedom she is seeking can only be found in Him. Jesus is her ANSWER! *"He is the Way, the Truth, and the Life..."* (John 14:6). Someone needs to tell Lori the truth, and I am surmising that that someone is me. Whew!

I've never been here before. This is unfamiliar territory, uncharted waters, "deep waters". A life is in peril. How can I ignore her silent plea of, "Help me, I'm drowning!"? What am I to do? She is drowning in despair, trapped by deception, entangled by years of abuse and if someone doesn't try to help her...

Thus a confrontation surges within. Waves of self-righteousness are washed away by compassion. Torrents of judgment are swept away by mercy. Tempests of lies are stilled by truth. Currents of fear are swallowed by faith.

135

Okay Lord! At your request I'm going in after her...

I'm trying to remember how this particular conversation surfaced. Ah, yes...prayer. More specifically, there was an incident that had occurred the previous weekend. I remember there being a thunderstorm on Saturday night and I felt impressed by the Holy Spirit to pray for Lori. I hardly knew Lori, but I prayed for protection and God's blessings on her life. I remember looking at the clock and it was late.....around midnight. I had recently been assigned temporarily to the same department in which Lori worked. At work the next week, I saw Lori and said "hello". To make small talk, I asked if she had had a good weekend. She began telling me about a car accident she was involved in on Saturday night and she barely escaped with her life. "You prayed for me!" she gasped. *Strange she would have known.* "As a matter of fact, I was praying for you on Saturday night," I replied. Lori's eyes glistened with amazement. "Thank God. I'm glad you're okay."

Sandi, my supervisor, with whom God had given me favor, overheard the conversation between Lori and me since we were standing in the doorway of her office. Lori was full of questions and wanted to continue the conversation. "Maybe during our lunch break," I thought. But when I looked at Lori, I knew she needed to talk *now!* The supervisor "busied" herself in order to grant me the time needed to dive into these troubled waters.

Hours passed as Lori shared her sordid past: the painful years of abuse while moving from one foster home to another; the years of teenage rebellion; the raping and beatings by her cruel stepfather whom she hoped was now "dead and in hell"; and multiple betrayals by church leaders who she thought she could trust. She had lived so many years in the icy, turbulent waters of emotional, physical and sexual abuse. She had tried desperately to swim out, only to be pulled under by stronger crashing waves of despondency. And now, she occupied the murky waters of lesbianism. These bleak waters seemed much warmer, kinder, and accepting, so she decided to tread there. Lori's tone of voice softened as she talked lovingly about sharing a life together with her partner, Melissa. Totally out of my element and shocked beyond belief, I listened while Lori continued chronicling the agonizing events that transpired throughout her adolescent years. I wasn't sure if she was trying to convince herself or convince me as she proceeded to talk about how happy she was now, and how lucky she was to have found Melissa and how much they really loved each other. She didn't think of herself as a bad person and then, pausing, told me she believed in God.

Oh my, she doesn't know the danger beneath the under currents. She can't stay here; she'll perish in these waters!

"Do you not know that the unrighteous will not inherit the kingdom of God? Do not be deceived. Neither fornicators, nor idolaters, nor adulterers, nor homosexuals, nor sodomites, nor thieves, nor covetous, nor drunkards, nor slanderers, nor

138

swindlers will inherit the kingdom of God."
(1 Corinthians 6:9-10)

My heart broke for Lori. I knew the timing of our meeting was critical. She was nearly killed in a recent car accident, but God's mercy intervened. This is the only night I am scheduled to work with her; and I knew in my heart this was not a coincidence but a divine appointment. With a nod of approval from my supervisor, I opened my Bible at the work station. "Holy Spirit, speak through me.....teach through me," I silently prayed. I began by apologizing to Lori on behalf of every church leader and Christian who had ever hurt or betrayed her. I hugged her and told her I loved her but more importantly, God loved her. And He wanted me to share truth with her according to His infallible Word. So for the next few hours we poured over God's Word. The Holy Spirit led me to specific scriptures pertaining to the truth regarding sexual immorality and its consequences, and God's initial plan for our lives and the plan of salvation. (Genesis 1:26-28; Leviticus 18:22;

139

Isaiah 53:5; Matthew 27:17-54; John 3:16; John 8:36, 44-45; Romans 1:18-32; Romans 3:23; Romans 12:1-2; 1 Corinthians 6: 18-20; 2 Corinthians 5:17; Galatians 5:19-21; Ephesians 5:3-7; Colossians 3:5-7; 1 Thessalonians 4:3-5; Revelations 3:20; Revelations 21:8; Revelations 22:15.)

Lori had so many questions. And while I understood the reasons why Lori had become involved in this homosexual lifestyle, I could not condone it. My opinions and thoughts were not pertinent to the issue. What she needed at this very moment was truth and not compromise. She needed truth, not pity. She needed truth, not self-righteous judgment. She needed Jesus! *"He is the Way, the Truth and the Life."* (John 14:6).

We were interrupted by Sandi, who informed us the end of the work shift would be over within thirty minutes. I prayed with Lori and explained to her how important it was for her to make a lifestyle change and reminded her of how much God loved her. He had made provision through His Son Jesus, and was offering a way out of these stagnant waters of lesbianism. She could be free, but it was her choice and I strongly encouraged her to choose a life in Christ.

Sandi, who had been standing in the doorway, smiled at me with tearful eyes and I thanked her for she too had been used by God in this rescue mission.

I did not cross paths with Lori again, so I don't know what decision she ultimately made. But I do know this. In Isaiah 55:11 God says, *"So shall My Word be that goes forth from My mouth; it shall not return to Me void, but shall accomplish what I please, and it shall prosper in the thing for which I sent it."* These were waters in which I had no idea I would ever venture into. I certainly am not a "certified lifeguard" nor am I capable of "saving" anyone. I realize now God did not expect me to save Lori but to show her the way out of these waters and offer her His "life vest".

My Friend, if by chance you happen upon someone drowning in despair or perhaps someone struggling in troubled waters please don't turn away. My hope is that you: will cast aside your personal and perhaps, judgmental opinions; will care enough to risk your discomfort, reputation or your position; will convey the love of Christ, allowing His compassion to swell in your heart; and will make a bold, life-changing decision to go in after her.

Not a strong swimmer? That's okay. Swim out as far as you can and then toss her the **Life Preserver**!

God will mend a broken heart if you give Him
all the pieces.

Aesop

Teresa L. Colbert

All Shook Up

Take an uninterrupted nap...

Settle in for a movie marathon...

Go for a scenic drive...

Curl up with a classic book...

Stroll in the park...

Sunday afternoons. Don't you just love them? It's time to get comfy, take off the dress and heels, and put on a pair of shorts or sweats. Like a kitten basking on a sunny window sill, I settle in for some "me time". Doing what I want, if I want, when I want. Sounds nice, doesn't it?

It's a perfect 70 degrees outside. A slight breeze wafts through the open window. The last I remember about the movie before reaching for the yellow crocheted afghan was: the young woman moving to England to embark upon a career in theater; her meeting a handsome, mysterious stranger on the train and them sitting together drinking coffee at a quaint café.

The tranquil effect of the curtains blowing in the breeze and the soft, cuddling of the crocheted afghan prevailed. (No wonder kittens purr.)

UGH! I forgot to shut off the one thing that interrupts a perfectly relaxing Sunday afternoon. RING! RING! RING! RING!

Well, it was nice while it lasted.

It's a call for prayer. I'm not sure how it happens, but I seem to always have energy to answer a call or request for prayer.

"If My people who are called by My name will humble themselves, and pray and seek My face, and turn from their wicked ways, then I will hear from heaven, and will forgive their sin and heal their land. Now My eyes will be open and My ears attentive to prayer made in this place." (2 Chronicles 7:14-15)

Having a little talk with Jesus is more refreshing than a Sunday afternoon nap!

Dwight, a member of our church prayer group, received a call with a request for prayer at Raymond's home. Very little information was given.... Raymond? A name, I didn't recognize. Maybe he's an extended family member, a former classmate or colleague that someone from the prayer group knows. I don't know. God knows. Now where did I put my car keys?

Wow, judging by the number of vehicles parked at Raymond's house, we were not the only Sunday afternoon visitors. Raymond's wife, Naomi was busy greeting friends and family and refilling trays of finger foods. She confirmed what we had suspected. There were several people from their church visiting with Raymond in the den. We waited while she went to tell him of our arrival. She returned and told us we were welcome to join Raymond and the others for prayer.

I've never met Raymond and Naomi, nor have I ever been in their home and yet I find myself assertively telling her, "No, we will wait. Allow your church group to finish their visit and then we will visit with your husband afterwards." Dwight and members of our prayer group looked questioningly at me. I did not know why, but I felt strongly we weren't supposed to join in with the other group. So we waited...

Minutes later, the door opened and we stood back as several ladies emerged from the den. Immaculately dressed in an array of colors, it was "interesting" to watch them parade one by one. The lady in lilac wore a matching hat and smiled faintly as she passed by. The lady with salt and pepper hair frantically searched her purse for keys. The next one wore a pale blue designer's suit and carried a Bible. The woman in the pink sleeveless dress assumed Dwight was a pastor and asked the name of our church. The lady wearing the yellow floral dress with black stiletto heels walked hurriedly past us, talking on her cell phone while two other women lingered whispering among themselves.

(Okay, humor me. One of my favorite past times is "people watching". I find them rather "interesting.")

Raymond was sitting comfortably on the sofa as we entered the den. He stood to greet us before engaging in small talk and catching up on family news. The noisy chatter in the hallway soon diminished and Dwight geared the conversation towards the reason for our visit. I was the only "newcomer' of the group, so Dwight asked me to introduce myself. Directing my attention towards Raymond I said, "Hi, my name is Ry'ah and I am absolutely certain God hears me when I pray!"

(Don't ask me why I interjected that piece of information. I have no idea. But I went on to say, Dwight, before we continue Raymond's wife needs to join us.")

While a member of our prayer group went to retrieve Naomi, Dwight asked Raymond to tell us about his recent doctor's visit. "Well, it wasn't the best news. I knew I was sick, but I had no idea it was this serious." He was told his heart condition was severe. It was highly unlikely he would ever work again. He was also told he would need a heart transplant and most likely would take medication for the rest of his life. He would be given a regimen of tests to determine his candidacy for a heart transplant and then there were no guarantees. Basically, the doctors gave him very little hope.

Naomi must have wondered why she had been requested to join us. The previous prayer group had not done so. Besides, she was much too busy playing hostess and after all, weren't we here to visit with Raymond? He was the one who needed prayer. Okay, sure she would join us for a quick prayer and scripture reading. This wouldn't take too long. The previous group was finished within fifteen minutes. Naomi sat by her husband and convincingly played the role of the supportive wife. She reiterated, "How sweet it was of us to come."

Remember me telling you how God sometimes tends to do the unthinkable, unimaginable and the incredible? None of us were prepared for what happened next as once again God decided to do the unexpected.

Years ago, there was a catchy advertising slogan, *"When E.F. Hutton speaks, people listen...."* While some may have indeed given ear to Mr. Hutton, I can assure you when the Spirit of God speaks, let's just say, HE has a captive audience! Oh and by the way, when HE speaks there absolutely will not be any:

- yawning or nodding off to sleep.
- fidgeting or doodling.
- daydreaming or interrupting.
- potty or smoke breaks allowed.

The Spirit of God began to reveal deep and secret things with such intensity declaring:

There were not one, but two serious heart conditions within the room and one was deemed more serious than the other. Raymond needed a heart transplant, but Naomi needed a change of heart. Raymond had a temporal condition, while Naomi's condition was an eternal one.

"...For the LORD searches all hearts and understands all the intent of the thoughts." (1 Chronicles 28:9)

HE continued exposing her hidden motives, prideful acts and manipulative behavior.

Underneath the smiles and pleasantries, Naomi's heart was full of bitterness and contempt.

She, as well as the rest of us, was astonished to say the least. We knew beyond a shadow of a doubt that everything which was spoken and revealed was done by the Spirit of God. For how else could a stranger make known the secret things embedded in her heart?

152

The masquerade was finally over; the mask had been removed and Naomi's heart was laid bare. In a state of brokenness and a spirit of repentance, Naomi sobbed as the love of God penetrated her heart.

Watching her reminded me of the times in my own life when I too needed a special touch from God. For I once harbored dark and unlovable things in my own heart.

What about you? What's your story? Have you encountered the love of God and thus had a change of heart? Do you remember when God exchanged your haughtiness for humility; replaced your fear with faith; and removed your guilt with grace?

I like the way Jeremiah tells it.

"The word which came to Jeremiah from the LORD, saying: "Arise and go down to the potter's house, and there I will cause you to hear my words." Then I went down to the potter's house, and there he was, making something at the wheel. And the vessel that he made of clay was marred in the hand of the potter; so he made it again into another vessel, as it seemed good to the potter to make." (Jeremiah 18:1-4)

Naomi and Raymond held each other in a loving embrace, and all was forgiven. Once again, God had done the unimaginable, unthinkable and incredible! Yet He wasn't quite finished as there was another heart condition which needed immediate attention.

Do you recall sitting in the waiting room and finally hearing, "next" or "the doctor will see you now"?

Raymond had patiently waited. Did he dare hope for another miracle?

If Naomi's heart had been the one deemed "more serious," then what could he hope to receive? At best, maybe, a confirmed candidacy for a transplant. He had no idea what to expect because this was not an ordinary prayer meeting, certainly not like any he had ever encountered.

As we gathered around and placed our hands on Raymond, each of us targeted special areas in prayer. We prayed earnestly for the medical team, specifically for an increase of Raymond's faith. Took authority over any fear, doubt or unbelief and praised God for His healing power. Being led of the Holy Spirit, I kneeled and placed my hands on Raymond's right calf and continued praying in the Spirit. The Spirit of God touched him and he began to shake, first his right leg and then his whole body shook with such force it seemed as though the whole room was shaking.

155

(If you are trying to figure this one out, it was new for me too. Then I happened upon this scripture).

> *"And when they had prayed, the place where they were assembled together was shaken; and they were all filled with the Holy Spirit, and they spoke the word of God with boldness."* (Acts 4:31)

Within I heard the words, **"Tell him"**. "No Lord, I can't. It would mean putting everything on the line." **"That's exactly what I want you to do, put everything, all of your faith, on the line,"** HE said. So in obedience to the Lord I told Raymond, "Tomorrow, request that your doctors conduct one more test. The test will confirm you are healed and have no need of a heart transplant, nor any medication."

On the drive home from work, I envisioned a relaxing evening with a bubble bath, soft music and popcorn for dinner. Thank goodness, there were no meetings to attend, no errands to run and no laundry to do! It had been a long, hectic and mentally draining day! The sofa looked too inviting to pass up, so the bubble bath would have to wait.

Don't you just hate it (well maybe hate is too strong a word to use) when you are awakened from a deep sleep and find yourself in a stupor?

You are awakened to a familiar noise but can't readily determine whether it is an alarm clock, telephone ringing, smoke detector, doorbell or the TV? So in a dazed process of elimination, you conclude it isn't the TV because the screen is blank. You pick up the telephone, say "hello" only to hear a dial tone. The alarm clock is in the bedroom and the sound is much closer. The smoke detector is loud enough to wake up the dead, so it must be the doorbell!

Dwight and his wife stood waiting. I quickly glanced at my watch which read 6:45. Surely I hadn't forgotten a meeting, had I? The voicemail! I had not checked the voicemail. How long had they been ringing the doorbell? After shaking the cobwebs from my brain, I opened the door and invited them in.

Dwight began, "We won't take much of your time, but we wanted to come and tell you the news. After completing a series of additional medical tests, the doctors have confirmed Raymond will not need a heart transplant and have taken him off all medication! "

Excuse me Friend, but right now, there's a praise party going on at 116 Oakhurst. Join me, won't you?

"Praise the LORD.

Praise God in his sanctuary;
praise him in his mighty heavens.
Praise him for his acts of power;
praise him for his surpassing greatness.
Praise him with the sounding of the trumpet,
praise him with the harp and lyre,
praise him with timbrel and dancing,

praise him with the strings and pipe,

praise him with the clash of cymbals,

praise him with resounding cymbals.

Let everything that has breath praise the LORD.

Praise the LORD." *(Psalm 150)*

"Never miss a good chance to shut up."

Will Rogers

Shut Up, Flesh!

Rain, again? So this is the 20% chance they predicted, huh? Actually more like a torrential downpour, if you ask me! Ducks wouldn't be caught out in this weather. They would have cancelled this Friday night appointment! Oh no, but not me. I'm out in this monsoon because good old me just had to say yes! I gave my word... yeah I gave my word alright, albeit regrettably. Surely this can't be what Jesus meant when He said, *"...If anyone desires to come after Me, let him deny himself, and take up his cross daily, and follow Me."* (Luke 9:23)

Follow Me? Well, I had no idea "follow me" would mean driving on dark country roads with no street lights, in the pouring rain, dodging potholes! It was windy and cold – the windshield wipers struggled to contend with the battering rain ...couldn't I have one, just one relaxing evening to myself? Ah, what I wouldn't give for a nice candlelit bubble bath to help ease the tension in my neck and head right now. Most sensible people are at home, heeding the advice of the meteorologists to stay inside avoiding this torrential downpour, but not me! "Ugh! Stupid dog," I screamed as a collie suddenly darted across the road, causing me to slam on the brakes and skid, missing a mailbox, but hitting a pothole...how much further? I felt a slight headache coming on... It had been a long week and now I could look forward to an even longer evening!

Yeah, my flesh was having its typical "meltdown"...the one it has when it's struggling to die. The one it has when I want my way, when I think I know best, when my comfort zone is stretched and I mean s-t-r-e-t-c-h-e-d! But then another inner voice interrupts, **"she is waiting for you. Remember she told Dan about you?"** Then, I'm reminded of a passage of scripture I read some time ago: *"...When you are old, you will stretch out your hands, and another will gird you and carry you where you do not wish."* (John 21:18). There is nothing quite like the gentle "attitude adjustment" of the Holy Spirit to steer you back on course. "Yes Lord, I know. Please forgive me," I said sighing, while rubbing the back of my neck. Stress had maneuvered its way into the car beside me, but soon exited as I submitted my will to His and the peace of God accompanied me for the remainder of the ride.

Rose, who had been employed with SPTB Electronics for nearly twenty years, worked in the quality assurance department. Apparently, earlier in the week, she overheard me sharing my testimony with another coworker during an evening break. I hadn't realized how intently she had been listening to my conversation until she spoke of how my face seemed to light up when I talked about the Lord and how she could listen to me talk about Him for hours. She commented on how warm and fuzzy it made her feel on the inside. That was a real compliment coming from Rose who rarely smiled and spent a lot of time complaining. Every day there was some complaint about the workload, new assignments, changes needed in management, or that the office was too hot or too cold. She was definitely an "unhappy camper."

So imagine my surprise when she excitedly tells me, "I told Dan, my husband, about you. I talked about you most of the weekend and he wants to meet you! Can you come to dinner on Friday night?"

"Well, uh, uh I guess I can?" I replied.

"Now we are not fancy people, just plain folk," Rose clarified. "I'm so excited and Dan will be thrilled you're coming too! I'll meet you at the Country Store which is about a half of a mile from our house."

Excuse me, but are you as confused as I am right now? How did a private conversation between me and another co-worker surface into Rose's living room over the weekend? What could she have possibly said that consequently intrigued Dan enough to invite me to dinner? So let's contemplate and see if we can make any sense out of this unusual occurrence.

1.   Friday, during the lunch hour, Lorraine, a co-worker, and I were seated at a table in the cafeteria. We were discussing weekend plans and I made mention of my plans to attend church on Sunday. Lorraine then asked me about my faith, which led to my talking about how I came to know the Lord Jesus as my Savior. We exhausted the entire lunch hour enthralled in this discussion.

2.   I noticed Rose as she entered the cafeteria. Her usual practice was to get a large glass of iced tea and then return to her desk to eat lunch and browse through Avon catalogs.

3.   Usually on Fridays, most employees ran errands or went out for lunch, hence, the noise level and seating availability made the cafeteria more inviting. It is possible while Lorraine and I were excitedly conversing (*Did I mention I have a tendency to talk with my hands?*) Rose decided to sit at one of the vacant tables nearby.

4.   *Sound plausible?* Well, if she did then, that would explain how she became privy to

private dialogue. It is true when I talk about my relationship, my love for Jesus, I get excited! I can't help it! The joy of the Lord seems to flow out of me. I can't fully explain it and I can't contain it! Rose must have witnessed it. That being the case, I may have misjudged her. Instead of eavesdropping, she was being drawn! She wasn't listening to gossip; she was hearing the Good News! She wasn't mishandling personal information; she was on a fact finding mission to discover the Truth!

I imagine there must have been something very different about Rose when she came home from work on Friday evening. I wonder if it was the excitement in her voice, or the amazement in her face, or the spring in her step or the absence of animosity. There was undoubtedly such a noticeable change in Rose that it piqued Dan's curiosity. In my mind's eye, I liken Rose's excitement to the incident that transpired nearly 2000 years ago. Remember the scene? The woman at the well, who after having such an inspiring encounter with Jesus, left her water pot, went running, exclaiming, *"Come, see a man..."* (John 4:29).

Maybe there is a more defined or, better yet, a "Divine" reason for this meeting. Just for the record, let's call this a "Divine Appointment". After all, we can't begin to use our finite minds to explain the how and the why of God's divine plans. I remember reading; *"For My thoughts are not your thoughts, nor are your ways my ways, says the Lord. For as the heavens are higher than the earth. So are my ways higher than your ways and my thoughts than your thoughts".* (Isaiah 55:8, 9)

I'm not sure why I accepted her invitation. Maybe it was her white hair. (After all, I was raised to be nice and respectful to my elders.) Maybe it was the sound of hope in her voice. (I was afraid of disappointing her.) Maybe it was the gleam in her eyes that tugged on my heart or maybe it was because I was caught off-guard and didn't know what else to say.

Whatever the reason, I took the bait, hook, line and sinker. Rose chattered excitedly as she gave me interesting directions to her house, which by the way, is one-half mile from the country store!

"Lord, why this particular evening?" I had no idea Rose lived out in "no man's land"! "I wonder if I am the only invited guest. What exactly am I supposed to say?" Ugh! Another pothole! Finally, yep, there it is: the country store, a half-mile from their house. The battle of my will succumbs to His silence; my flesh bows to His Lordship. "Yes, Lord!" Whether rain or shine, country roads or city streets, tired or refreshed........I promised I would go through any door you opened. And a promise is a promise. "Watch out for the pothole! Shut up flesh!"

Rose's face beamed as she introduced me to her husband, Dan. She suggested we get acquainted while she prepared dinner. "Okay, Lord. Now what?" Dan obviously was the "appointment". **"You're the first Black person to visit their house"** the Holy Spirit informed me. Dan and I made small talk, but at times his nervousness was quite evident. Surely, Rose had made mention of my skin color, or maybe not.

169

Dear Friend, I often wonder if the day will ever come when the color of one's skin will cease to be an issue, when prejudice will become as obsolete as the dinosaur, and when the truth of God's word will prevail in the heart of mankind.

"There is neither Jew nor Greek, there is neither slave nor free, there is neither male nor female; for you are all one in Christ Jesus." (Galatians 3:28)

No matter, God had a specific plan for this evening and apparently I was to play a key role in it. I soon found a comfortable topic of interest for Dan when I asked about his children and grandchildren. He proudly showed family photos and told special stories about the grandchildren. Shortly thereafter, Rose announced dinner was ready. We gathered around their small kitchen table as Rose served fish and chips, coleslaw and iced tea.

During the conversation at dinner, I learned Dan had been deeply hurt by a church leader nearly twenty years earlier and while the wound had scabbed over, it was very apparent by the tone of his voice that this remained a sensitive area. Dan practically dropped his fork when I agreed he had been wronged and then proceeded to apologize for the wrong that had been done to him. Someone in my "family" had grossly offended him... twenty years is much too long for anyone to bear any burden... so yes, I apologized sincerely and profusely. Dan needed to move on...to get past... *"forgetting those things which are behind and reaching forward to those things which are ahead."* (Philippians 3:13) So there was no more talk of church or religion... there was no need to continue pouring salt into the wound when the "Balm of Gilead" was readily available for healing.

Dear Friend, you should have seen the incredulous look on Rose's face when I agreed that Dan shouldn't go back to church; he didn't need religion and he was just as good as the rest of them!

After a few moments of utter silence and looks of disbelief.... gave them time to sink their teeth into these profound possibilities...

- "Don't go back to church Dan, go to Jesus!"
- "You don't need religion, you need a relationship!"
- *"...There is none righteous, no, not one."* (Romans 3:10)

With their interest piqued, I proceeded to talk about this amazing relationship I have with Jesus, how HE also desired to have a relationship with Dan.... How Jesus hadn't hurt him but loved him. We also discussed how Jesus had led me from the mountains of North Carolina to Sparta...the likelihood of my working at the same company within the same department, meeting Rose and how He, Jesus, sent me out on this stormy night to their house to eat fish and chips knowing I am not a seafood lover!

Then the mood of the evening had lightened, and Rose suggested we convene in the living room to talk further and leave the dishes for later. Time passed so quickly and it was 10:00 p.m. before we knew it! Throughout the evening, God had quietly begun a work in Dan and skin color was no longer an issue. He was being drawn by the Spirit of God and listened intently as I shared about this wonderful relationship with Jesus. As the evening came to a close, with their permission, I prayed over their home and their family and thanked God for the honor of meeting them.

At work on Monday, Rose was still beaming. Dan had talked about that evening the entire weekend and would love for me to visit again. "I have never seen him like this," Rose said. "He has been smiling and whistling and talking my 'ears off'," laughed Rose. "The two of us went out to dinner last night. We haven't done that in years!"

One of the most endearing passages in the Bible is the parable of the Good Shepherd leaving the ninety-nine sheep to go after the one sheep and restore him to the sheepfold.

"What man of you, having a hundred sheep, if he loses one of them, does not leave the ninety-nine in the wilderness, and go after the one which is lost until he finds it? And when he has found it, he lays it on his shoulders, rejoicing. And when he comes home, he calls together his friends and neighbors, saying to them, 'Rejoice with me, for I have found my sheep which was lost!" (Luke 15:4-6)

This scene is replayed in my mind as I sat in a small country church watching a man who had sworn he would never step foot inside a church building again, beaming with joy. Over the past weeks I had eaten dinner and shared genuine conversation with a man who had struggled with racism and religion. And now he had grown to love and respect the Christ in me. The love of God can warm the coldest of hearts and I'm watching this miracle unfold before my eyes.

Tonight, at Dan's invitation, I am attending a Christmas pageant in which he is performing the role of Joseph.

Dear Friend, may I remind you that this is the same man who swore he "would never step foot in church again!"

After a marvelous performance, the audience applauded as the cast took their bows. Rose and I looked questioningly at each other when Dan asked permission to say a few words. He spoke of how his life had changed during the past months, and how he had been away from God and the church for the past twenty years. He humbly thanked God for His forgiveness. He told of how God had brought this little "colored girl" into his life to show him what he needed. And now he understood the difference between "being religious" and having a relationship with Jesus Christ. He rededicated his life to Christ and requested to be baptized again! "And if it wouldn't be too much trouble, preacher, can we do it right here, right now?" Rose reached over and squeezed my hand as tears of joy streaked her face. I kept trying to swallow the lump in my throat as my heart was overflowing with thanksgiving.

Guess what? On the way home, I find myself once again driving on country roads in the pouring rain, dodging potholes with no street lights and it's cold and windy. Forgive me, but I'm having another flesh meltdown, not grumbling, but grateful, not complaining, but crying tears of joy.

"Men never do evil so completely and
cheerfully as when they do it from a religious
conviction."

Blaise Pascal

Teresa L. Colbert

Shark Attack!

I couldn't believe what I was hearing. My heart gripped with anguish as I listened to fellow co-workers, "professing Christians", spewing venomous insults that would have received the approval and applause from hell. The snarled looks on their faces took on the persona of an angry, murderous mob. Aren't these the same people who faithfully attend church, sing in the choir and teach Sunday school? Yet, as the venom continued and the rage intensified, I wondered if this mirrored the scene that took place over 2000 years ago with those religious folks who cried, "Crucify Him!", "Crucify Him!" Dear Lord, have mercy! Please deliver me from these dangerous waters where I find myself surrounded by sharks and swarmed by piranhas......Had I been here all along? Are they a reflection of my own heart?

"...For out of the abundance of the heart, the mouth speaks." (Luke 6:45)

"Death and life are in the power of the tongue..." (Proverbs 18:21)

Forgive me Lord! I feel so dirty...I think I understand and agree with Isaiah: Woe is me! I am a woman of unclean lips and I am in the midst of an unclean people! Cleanse me! Change me! Lord.

The bitter gossip continued as torrents of hatred and prejudice filled the office atmosphere. Ken was today's bait for the piranhas in the office. Ken, I learned, was a co-worker who was suspected of being a homosexual and having contracted AIDS. He had been out on medical leave and returned to work last week. I had been reassigned to work the 7 p.m. shift and my flesh had something to say about it. "UGH!!!! Just my luck! Why me? What am I supposed to be, a night owl? I have a college degree...what am I doing working the night shift?" Oh well, it's only for the month of February. I tried to convince myself the time would pass quickly, but little did I know this fish would be swimming upstream for months to come.

One evening during a shift change in the locker room, a guy with red hair came in.

"Hi," he said.

"Hello, my name is Ry'ah," I said.

"My name is Ken."

Now what are the chances that out of the thousands of employees at this company, I would meet Ken in the locker room? Could this be *THE* Ken? In all of the spewed venom a description of him was never given. This couldn't possibly be the same person the office piranhas were attacking! He seems like such a nice guy. And by the way, where is everyone? Typically, this change room is like a beehive buzzing with activity. People are constantly coming and going. But right now, at this moment, only Ken and I are here. Yes, you got it...this was the "Ken" and that explains why the locker room was vacant.

As I was trying to put two and two together, Ken began to tell me, a stranger, about his life! Go figure! Wait a minute! We've just met! This water is WAY TOO DEEP! Jesus, please help me! Then that taunting, mocking, irritating voice whispers... you know, the same one who beguiled Eve...the

181

one who speaks lies, promotes fear and orchestrates confusion.

"Remember, you're the girl from the close-knit community..... You don't know anything about 'his kind'.... After all, he's only reaping what he has sown...that's what the Bible says, right?"

Ken, a young man in his late thirties, was a former school teacher. His face lit up as he recalled his days in the classroom and it was apparent he still missed that part of his life. Years ago he had been in the "party" scene and lived a wild and reckless life. Yes, it was true he had contracted the dreaded disease. Last August, he had participated in an experimental test group for people with AIDS. The prognosis did not look good and he was told he would probably not live through December. Five of the members of the test group had already lost their battle to AIDS, but somehow and for some reason, Ken was still alive. The cocktail of medicines was not guaranteed to cure him, but could help prolong his life. He attributed it to luck. I smiled...knowingly... No Ken, not by luck, but by divine intervention and our meeting is by divine appointment.

We were both blind... both bound; I by self-righteousness, and Ken by condemnation. This "saved" and "self-righteous" girl was in dire need of a divine appointment with the grace of God and this reminder: *"For by grace you have been saved through faith, and that not of yourselves; it is the gift of God."* (Ephesians 2:8)

(Now there's nothing quite like a good 'ole swift kick in your self righteousness to put you back on track.)

After I shared the good news of the Gospel with Ken and how much Jesus loved him, his eyes filled with tears and asked if Jesus could really love him, an AIDS victim. "Yes, Ken!"

"...Those who are well have no need of a physician, but those who are sick. I did not come to call the righteous, but sinners, unto repentance." (Mark 2:17) The bench in a locker room became an altar as I prayed with Ken to commit his life to Christ. As the angels in heaven

183

rejoiced, I gave my brother a hug and welcomed him into the family of God.

Previously, during another verbal episode of "stoning" Ken, the Holy Spirit spoke through me and challenged the "office piranhas". *"He who is without sin among you, let him throw a stone…"* (John 8:7) We were reminded *"for all have sinned and fall short of the glory of God."* (Romans 3:23).

Discussions erupted regarding the hatred of sin, but loving the sinner and the seven things the Lord hates:

"A proud look

A lying tongue

Hands that shed innocent blood

A heart that devises wicked plans

Feet that are swift in running to evil

A false witness who speaks lies and

One who sows discord among the brethren."

(Proverbs 6:17-19)

I can't speak for the others, but the Word of God penetrated my heart and birthed a friendship with Ken, my newfound brother in Christ. By God's grace, I was being delivered from the gross sins of hypocrisy and prejudice while His love was being worked in me and through me. As days passed, the blatant slander quieted to derogatory murmurs. It was now clear to me why I had been placed on the 7 p.m. shift. God knew I needed a "Ken" encounter for my spiritual growth and Ken needed to encounter and experience the "love of Jesus". Wow! It is very humbling when the Father reveals those dark places in your heart and gives you an opportunity to allow the light of His love to shine through.

Ken and I stayed in touch via email or in passing during shift changes. He never commented on the cold treatment, the glaring looks or the snickering he continued to receive from other co-workers. He was grateful for each day and thankful for God's provision through this job. Due to the astronomical cost of his medical treatments, Ken had to give up his house and move in with his dad. Still his attitude remained positive as his faith in God continued to grow.

The next week seemed quite unusual:

185

Monday - No word from Ken, so I emailed him.

Tuesday - No email from Ken, which was so unlike him.

Wednesday - I called, only to get his voicemail (I was getting a little concerned).

Thursday - Still no word from him and I didn't see him during the shift change.

On Friday - I expressed my concern regarding Ken to our Supervisor.

She agreed this was unusual behavior for Ken and decided to call him at home. After a dozen or so rings, a faint voice answered. "Ken, this is Sandi and Ry'ah. Are you all right?" Ken told us he had fallen three days ago and was unable to get up. Somehow he had managed to crawl over to the telephone. He cried as he embarrassingly explained he had soiled his clothing. Sandi called 911 and requested assistance for Ken. I was under the impression Ken lived with this dad, so where was he? "Lord please don't let Ken die alone...that would be dreadful. If there is no one else, I'd like to be there whenever his time comes."

There were many concerns and unanswered questions that prompted a drive to Ken's house. It was a long, although pretty drive to the rural area of Cedar Grove...miles and miles of rolling farmland, beautiful oak, maple trees and endless fields of wildflowers. "Picturesque, but much too rural for me," I thought as I drove along on the partly graveled, partly paved winding road. Other than the occasional vehicle passing, I didn't see any other activity and was somewhat anxious to arrive at my destination. According to the directions, I was to continue driving five more miles and turn left onto a dirt road. Ken and his dad lived in an old single wide trailer. I knocked on the door and was met by a man with a dark, menacing look in his eyes. For a moment, I was convinced I was looking directly into the face of Satan himself. His continuing cold stare sent shivers down my spine as I faced this intimidating spirit. Then I was reminded by the Holy Spirit, *"He who is in you is greater than he who is in the world..."* (1John 4:4) *"For God has not given us a spirit of fear, but of power and of love and of a sound mind."* (2 Timothy 1:7)

A sigh of relief spilled forth as the Holy Spirit reminded me of who I was and more importantly, *whose* I was. "Hello, I am a co-worker of Ken's. Is he at home?" The man frowned, mumbled a few words and pointed to Ken who was lying in a hospital bed asleep. To my relief, he left abruptly, slamming the door behind him.

Faith, a hospice volunteer, greeted me as I entered the home. She and I talked quietly as she patiently answered my questions. Faith, a committed Christian, shared her love for Jesus and welcomed this opportunity to care for Ken. God let me know she was his "ram in the bush". She would be the one beside Ken's bedside during his final hours. Faith kept a journal in which she noted the activities, visitors, medications, requests and other information regarding Ken. I asked about Ken's dad and his absence during the time of Ken's fall.

Have mercy Lord! The harsh man at the door was Ken's dad she told me. He is an alcoholic… a mean, cruel, vindictive, man. During one of his most recent binges, he had beaten Ken with his fists. One evening, he brought his drunken buddies to the house to gawk at Ken while in a weakened state. They yelled, cursed and hurled insults, accusing him of being "less than a man." Ken's dad put a gun in his hand and encouraged Ken to kill himself.

Tears were stinging both of our eyes as Ken stirred in the bed across the room. Faith and I regained our composure as she tended to Ken's needs.

He was happy to see me and my usual question for him was, "What shall we talk to our FATHER about today?" I wasn't prepared for his answer. "I'm tired, Ry'ah. I'm ready...I want to go and live with Jesus.... pray He will take me home." I walked away from Ken's bed. No one had ever asked me to pray for them to die... I knew God could heal him....was it wrong to pray for death when God is the Giver of life? Torn between Ken's desire and my faith, I realized this choice wasn't mine to make. Ken was of sound mind, he was sure of his relationship with Jesus Christ and he was ready to close this chapter of his life and move on to the next one. "Dear God give me strength and the words ...pray through me Holy Spirit." I swallowed hard, fought back tears, took a deep breath and began... "Father, you've heard your son's request, the desire of his heart and his longing to be with you. I thank You Lord that Ken's name is written in the Lamb's Book of Life. Angels in heaven please prepare to receive this child of God. In the name of Jesus I pray, amen."

Ken was smiling contentedly as we finished praying and he thanked me for coming to visit him. He wouldn't be returning to work and asked me to say hello to Sandi, our supervisor, and others who were concerned about him. I left reassured that Faith would lovingly care for Ken and would keep me apprised of his condition.

Ken's health quickly took a turn for the worse. I received a call from Sandi with news that Ken was in the hospital. It wouldn't be long now. Upon entering Ken's room, the nurse cautioned me that he was heavily medicated and may not recognize me. She offered me plastic gloves and a mask, but I politely declined both.

As I approached Ken's bedside, she asked Ken if he recognized me. He reached for my hand, smiled and faintly said, "Yes, this is my angel!"

"Hi Ken, It's good to see you. What shall we talk to our FATHER about today?" I asked.

"I need pajamas," he said. "I can't meet Jesus in a hospital gown!"

"Yes, Ken. We will get pajamas for you," I replied.

"I thank God for you," he replied.

"No Ken, the honor has been mine. Say a special hello to Jesus for me, will you?" I asked. He gently squeezed my hand, the nurse smiled and I quietly left the room. A few days later, Ken went home to be with the Lord.

The sparse parking lot affirmed my suspicions there would only be few in attendance. Approaching the small brick church, I noticed a young lady standing in the breezeway quietly crying and being comforted by the pastor. A few minutes later, the pastor greeted me. He assured me no formal introduction was needed, for Ken had spoken of me in many of their conversations. We shared fond memories, talked of Ken's love for the Lord and I was then introduced to the woman standing in the breezeway.

She was Ken's sister! Wait a minute... Ken never mentioned he had a sister. My mind raced as I tried to process this "you've got to be kidding me" piece of news!

Why had he never mentioned her? Where had she been for the past two years? Had she known of his illness? Had she shunned him?

I guess, at this point, in the grand scheme of things, it really didn't matter. Ken was now resting in peace... his tedious journey was over...his prayer had been answered.

(Yeah, but come on, aren't you the least bit interested in the fact that after all this time, you are now being introduced to Ken's sister?) It's almost like coming to the end of a letter and

discovering there is a "p.s." Well I think we have just met the "p.s.", so apparently there is more to this assignment than first thought.

I told her about my two-year spiritual journey with her brother and how grateful I was for the opportunity to have known him. Overwhelmed with guilt and filled with remorse, the floodgates of her pent-up emotions soon erupted and spilled forth much like an overflowing riverbank. Growing up, she and Ken had been very close. Things changed after their mother's death...their dad's drinking, as well as his temper had escalated....she couldn't wait to leave home and when she did, she never came back. Though they had not spoken for a very long time, she had known about Ken's secret lifestyle...but she hadn't known about his illness... She thought about calling many times, but never got around to it... she was married....had a family.... And was fearful of telling her kids the truth about their Uncle Ken.....She regretted not having the courage to stand up to their alcoholic father; so she chose to stay away. If only she had called... If only she had known...If only she had known. "I loved my brother. I'm so sorry Kenny! Oh God, I'm so sorry," she sobbed.

This burden was much too heavy and she had carried it long enough. So, she and I did what her brother and I had done so many times before... We had a little talk with Jesus and told Him all about her troubles! And she too discovered a little talk with Jesus is just what she needed.

"Come to Me, all you who labor and are heavy laden, and I will give you rest." (Matthew 11:28)

Ken's life may have been short-lived, but his "home going" was a grand celebration! He had not dreaded this day, but joyfully awaited the day he would see Jesus. The Pastor commented about how he had never met anyone who welcomed death in an excited fashion as Ken had. No, this was not intended to be a sad occasion but a celebration. Ken's casket was overlaid with red and white carnations, white doves and bells commemorating his new life of peace and joy in Christ.

We said our goodbyes to Ken and rejoiced as this favorite passage of scripture was read in his memory:

"The Lord is my shepherd, I shall not want." *(He's taken care of everything!)*

"He makes me to lie down in green pastures;" *(Ah, much more comfortable than hospital beds.)*

"He leads me beside still waters. He restores my soul;" *(No more suffering.)*

"He leads me in the paths of righteousness for His name's sake.

Yea, though I walk through the valley of the shadow of death," *(AIDS free!)*

"I will fear no evil; for you are with me; Your rod and Your staff, they comfort me.

You prepare a table before me in the presence of my enemies:

You anoint my head with oil; my cup runs over". *(with unspeakable Joy)*

195

Surely goodness and mercy will follow me all the days of my life; and I will dwell in the house of the Lord forever." (Absent from the body, present with the Lord)

(Psalm 23)

Dear Friend, my life has been so enriched by this "Ken experience". My faith continues to grow as I move away from shallow waters and follow the Spirit's leading into the deep. My hope is if you should ever find yourself amid sharks and piranhas, if your heart has grown callous and cold in the stagnant waters of religion, if your appetite is whet by preying on the weak, this "Ken experience" will awaken and stir your heart to one of compassion for your fellow man.

For if we really take an honest moment to look back over our lives, bring the skeletons out of the closet and "remember when," we'll find our stories share the same headliners:

197

- *Lured by the Wrong Bait*
- *Caught in a Net of Sin and by the Grace of God*
- *Rescued from Polluted Waters*

The old folks often say, "You never really know much about a person until you walk a mile in their shoes." So come with me, there's someone, an unlikely sort, I'd like for you to meet. Meeting him changed my life, perhaps it will yours too.

Teresa L. Colbert

Angel Food

WILL WORK FOR FOOD, the sign read.

There was definitely something different about him or was it something different about me? This certainly wasn't the first time I had seen people standing on street corners holding up signs. Every once in a while, I'd perform my religious, "Good Samaritan" routine: whisper a quick prayer, give a few dollars and go on my merry way. So what's different about today? I don't know. Yet something unsettling is happening inside of me. Reflecting upon a familiar passage of scripture,

"Now Peter and John went up together to the temple at the hour of prayer, the ninth hour. And a certain man lame from his mother's womb was carried, whom they laid daily at the gate of the temple which is called Beautiful, to ask alms from those who entered the temple." (Acts 3: 1-2)

Many religious people hurriedly passed by the beggar daily, some on their way to prayer service, to and from the temple, doing good works, or on their way to the next appointment.

I found myself wondering how many times had I (we) passed by? How many times had I passed by totally self-absorbed with "what I should have for dinner," preoccupied with my upcoming weekend plans, talking on the cell phone, my mind on autopilot while driving my daily commute? How many times had I nonchalantly given a few dollars to appease my conscience? But not today! Today was *different*. What was it? Ah yes, a momentary struggle, a conflict of interest, a battle of my will..... "But the traffic is heavy.....this is a dangerous intersection, several fatalities recorded in recent months. There's no safe place to pull over." I was trying hard to convince myself this was sound logical reasoning and perhaps it was. Or was I doing what many of us do during these inner struggles? Justifying and making excuses. Maybe someone else will stop to help him. After all, he could be a scam artist. What about the local food pantries? But before I could come up with another rationalization, I was presented with another alternative. **"You give him something to eat"**...Oh my... could this be the same voice that gave the same instruction nearly 2000 years ago. Remember? The disciples suggested they send the hungry multitude away and Jesus said, "...*You give them something to eat*". (Mark 6:37) Or could this be a revelation to the prayer I had prayed days before? "Lord, please let me see people through your eyes and love them through your heart". With tears threatening to spill from my eyes, the Holy Spirit spoke to me and said, **"Give him something to eat, something healthy, no junk food".**

I looked at Marian, my roommate, and it was apparent the Holy Spirit had touched her heart as well. She confirmed the Lord was stirring and steering us in a different direction today. We drove in silence, listening for HIS voice, His instructions...and went in search of food...healthy food.

"I'd like a grilled chicken sandwich, a baked potato, and a bottle of water please." There was a twinge of excitement mixed with fear, and yet there was an overwhelming sense of peace. *I know this doesn't make sense, but let's just say it was a "God thing".* We knew we were being led by the Lord. His instructions had been clear, so this was definitely not the time for procrastinating or making excuses.

It was mid-August...a Sunday afternoon. Marian and I were driving home, reminiscing about our wonderful weekend visit with Jerry and Amber. They had grown so much in their Christian faith. They were using their gifts and talents for the kingdom of God and "bearing much fruit." Our time together had been filled with laughter, prayer, encouragement, and sharing God's word. The time had passed by much too quickly. After we said our goodbyes, Jerry and Amber exited onto I-40 East, and we went to Asheville Highway. And there he stood, with his backpack, holding a handmade sign that read, WILL WORK FOR FOOD. There was nothing unusual about his appearance: disheveled as you might expect, dirty jeans, rumpled shirt and scruffy beard.

But I tell you Friend there was something, "different" about him:

...something about him disrupted my train of thought,

...something about him overshadowed the melancholy of our friends' departure,

...something about him made me sit up and take notice.

So much so, that seeing him interrupted and brought our lively conversation to a speechless halt.

The traffic.... Where's the traffic? What traffic? Strange... there's no traffic. This is one of the busiest intersections at I-40. So, where is the traffic? I'd better hurry before the traffic...... "Sir! Sir! O Sir!" The stranger places the hand held sign on the ground, leaves his backpack, turns and walks towards me. I leave the car door open, just in case.

He carefully takes the bag of food extended to him and then he pauses and looks at me......directly at me. Some have since asked if I was afraid, but surprisingly, I was not. When I looked into his weathered and worn face, I did not see the hardened look of a criminal, no signs of apprehensiveness and to my amazement, no ramblings like that of a crazed addict. I beheld the face of a man with the kindest, most heartwarming, piercing, blue eyes I had ever seen. Behind those piercing deep blue eyes were the look of hope and civility.

The response from the man surprised me. "Thank you and God bless you". Pray for me".

"I will, we will," I say as I began walking towards the open car door.

"What's your name?" he asks following me to the car.

"My name is Ry'ah and this is Marian".

"My, my name is Michael... Pray for me" he implored.

Marian and I drive away in silence, not quite sure what has just occurred. I turn to look back.

Michael is sitting on the ground with his "healthy lunch" at the corner of this busy intersection as the traffic is now whizzing by. For what seemed to be a span of minutes, it appeared as though traffic had been re-routed, brought to a standstill, or diminished, if you will.

Would you agree this is a most peculiar day?

The tears that had threatened to spill over earlier are now running down our faces. And I'm reminded once again, that I've been in shallow water too long. "A launch into the deep" sometimes requires us to stop at a busy intersection to:

- share our bread with the hungry.
- help those who are in need.
- clothe the naked.
- extend ourselves to the destitute.

For Jesus himself, reminded us: *"...I was hungry and you gave Me food; I was thirsty and you gave Me drink; I was a stranger and you took*

Me in; I was naked and you clothed Me..." (Matthew 25:35-36)

"...Assuredly, I say to you, inasmuch as you did it to one of the least of these My brethren, you did it to Me." (Matthew 25:40).

For so many years, my faith has been anchored in shallow waters, but today I'm stepping into waters that are rising. No longer is the water ankle deep. For now it is rising beyond the knees, rising to waist level and becoming deeper. I sense this isn't my last time in these waters, nor will this be my last encounter with Michael.

Thoughts of him continued to swirl in my mind for days as I wondered: Who was he, really? What about family? Surely someone must be searching for him. How long had Michael been homeless? I dreaded the thought of him scavenging through dumpsters for food. Did he sleep under an overpass or tucked away somewhere in an alley? There are shelters... surely he sleeps at one of the local shelters...oh my.

I thought of how much in life I take for granted. Each day I awaken and arouse from having slept in a warm, comfortable bed. I have the privilege of walking into a kitchen that is amply supplied with my choice of food. I have a place to call "home", a comfort the "Michaels" of this world long for but are without.

I imagined Michael's mornings were quite different. Instead of arousing from a comfortable bed, he most likely slept on a hard floor or cold pavement. He has no cupboards to open, no refrigerator to scour and no hot shower to soothe his aching muscles. He gets up shivering, grabs his bedroll then scrounges in his backpack for any leftover remnants of food. Excuse his rumpled appearance. His crumpled clothes dub as pajamas. A disposable razor and hot water are not readily obtainable; so please overlook the scruffy beard and ignore the slight smell of body odor.

As you and I rush off to work, Michael stuffs his meager belongings into his backpack. He tucks the homemade "WILL WORK FOR FOOD" sign under his arm and begins his trek to the grassy corner adjacent the busy intersection. You and I anticipate having a good day at the office. Michael, well, he just hopes somebody will give him a chance to: eat at least one meal today; show he isn't looking for a handout, just a hand up; and demonstrate his worth.

And he is even more so optimistic that maybe, just maybe:

•   Bob, the gas station attendant, allows him the use of the restroom to "freshen up" a bit.

•   Ms. Ann, the cafeteria worker, remembers to set aside a plate of leftover food for him.

•   Janie, the library assistant, grants him permission to come inside - a short reprieve from the scorching heat.

Each day I prayed God would provide for Michael and protect him. I wondered if I should have done more. Maybe I should have taken the time to pray with him instead of focusing on the traffic of the busy intersection, or at least asked for his last name and maybe bought him more than one meal. Like I said before, there was something different about him. In any case, I was certain God was doing something different in me, teaching me, stretching me beyond the me, my, and I zones. Thank You Lord. I am seeing him through your eyes and heart.

After a long hard week at work, Marian and I were so relieved to see Friday afternoon and eager to get home and out of the pre-Labor Day weekend traffic. We carefully planned our homeward route, avoiding the heaviest traffic tie-ups and exited the highway.

Déjà' vu! There he was! Michael! Well, it certainly looked like him from a distance.

Okay Friend, change of plans...No longer homeward bound, we are going in search of "healthy food", just in case.

The line at the drive-thru was unbelievably long. I wasn't sure if these patrons were really hungry or just using this time as an escape from the heavy traffic. I was growing more impatient by the minute as cars moved at a snail's pace. We were on a mission and anxious for another opportunity to see Michael. Whew! In spite of the long delay at the drive-thru, stopped by several traffic lights and maneuvering through massive traffic, we finally arrived at the exit. It had to be Michael. The guy was sitting in the same grassy area as before. Had he been here all day? Had he gotten weak from standing in the hot sun? Had anyone bothered to stop? Had he gotten discouraged?

Oh my goodness! You are not going to believe this, Friend! As we returned with the food, the traffic was again minimal to say the least! I can't explain it. It is Friday evening, Labor Day weekend rush hour and traffic is almost non-existent!!!

"Michael! Michael!" The man turns, stands and starts walking towards me.

"How do you know my name?" he asks. "We've met before... I'm Ry'ah and this is Marian," I said, extending the bag of food to him.

"God bless you," he says.

"Michael, we have been praying for you. We would like to invite you to dinner on Labor Day."

"Labor Day," Michael repeated.

"Yes, Labor Day is Monday... We can meet you here at twelve o'clock on Monday and take you to our house. Would you like to come, Michael?" I asked.

"Yes... thank you," he replied.

"Okay then, we'll see you on Monday at twelve o'clock."

Traffic is now moving slowly as many onlookers are noticing Michael and me. A van with a family of four watched, smiled and then slowly drove away. A police car pulled over and I waved to assure the officer everything was fine. A driver of a SUV looked on, as did many others. I couldn't blame them though... It was 100 degrees and humid. Not to mention that a busy intersection is certainly not the most convenient place to "chit-chat". This scene would have made an interesting front page headliner: *The Odd Couple Meets and Greets at I-40.*

213

Oh I'm sure this made for an interesting conversation around the dinner table or made for office gossip. But I hope at least one person saw something more than an "odd couple," more than a homeless man and a black woman. I pray he or she saw a demonstration of kindness.

Dear Friend,

Kindness isn't always about convenience, cleanliness, and comfort. I am beginning to understand this Christian life is about living to bring glory and honor to God.

> *"Let your light so shine before men that they may see your good works and glorify your Father in heaven."* (Matthew 5:16)

We were so excited that Michael agreed to come. Now we could do more than hand him food at an intersection. We would cook and allow him to eat a meal at our table. We would take the time to find out more about Michael and ways we could be of help to him.

On Monday, we arrived early in case Michael was waiting for us. After nearly two hours of waiting and driving within the vicinity, to our disappointment, Michael never came. Had he forgotten? Had something happened to him? We had no way of knowing. We didn't know where else to look for him. We had no address nor did we know his last name. We were unaware of the fact that, oftentimes, a homeless person doesn't keep track of time nor know what day it is. For the next few weeks, we purposely drove by the area, hoping to see Michael and kept non-perishable food items and bottled water on hand, just in case. The grassy area at the corner of the busy intersection showed no signs of him, nor did the local convenience store parking lot or the area under the I-40 overpass. Regrettably, we never saw Michael again. I have often wondered why our time with him was brief and why the Labor Day appointment was cancelled.

Could it be our time with Michael was as the Apostle Paul described?

"Do not forget to entertain strangers, for by so doing, some have unwittingly entertained angels." (Hebrews 13:2)

Whether or not Michael was an angel, I don't know. But I do believe my encounters with him were by God's divine appointment and I believe one day, I'll cross paths with Michael again.

Dear Friend, the next time you stop at a busy intersection, look beyond the dirty jeans, the oily hair and the scruffy beard. Reach deeper than your wallet, disregard the traffic and set aside your personal agenda. Then maybe, just maybe, you too will be given an extraordinary opportunity to experience the heartbeat of God.

Sharing the Journey

Well my friend, you're quite the trooper! I must say, I am amazed at your perseverance. Not only did you climb the mountains of unforeseen challenges, forge through waters of unpredictability, and venture into unfamiliar territory, but you stayed the course.

Isn't it good to know you "can do all things through Christ who gives you strength"? (Philippians 4:13)

I am so glad you decided to join me. The journey is more enriching, and the memories are more special when you can share them. Thanks for:

* laughing with me when we hung out with Ma.
* crying with me at my Mother's grave.
* praying with me in the salon.

- sitting with me by Ken's bedside.
- rejoicing with me as we witnessed God's miraculous power.

It appears we'll be stopping here for a while beside the quiet waters. So please, by all means take this time to: check on the kids; toss in a load of laundry; run to the grocery store; or return phone calls.

Me? Oh, I'll be conferring with the Guide and awaiting His instructions for the next leg of the journey. So for now, I'll rest and wait with Him beside the quiet waters.

I'm looking forward to the exhilarating surprises, unspeakable joys and welcoming rays of triumphs. But they can only be encountered as we continue the journey. Care to join me?

Want to go further? Bring a friend. Invite your spouse. Yes, of course your Pastor is welcome to join us!

But before you go, I am curious to know your thoughts as you accompanied me on this journey beyond shallow waters. Please take a few moments to jot down your thoughts, special memories, faith-lessons learned and contact me @

tlcolbert.journey@gmail.com or

www.teresalcolbert.com.

Also follow me on twitter:

@Teresa_Colbert

Hey! Don't forget those souvenirs you picked up along the way. Be sure to share them with your family and friends.

Okay, I'll see you as we continue the journey.

Ry'ah

Souvenirs

from

THE JOURNEY...

BEYOND SHALLOW WATERS

The Guide is waiting. Be sure to stay close to Him, for He knows the way.

Look for God. Often times you may find Him in the most unconventional places.

Offer the Life Preserver to someone drowning in despair.

Go get your brother.
Galatians 6:1: *"Brethren, if a man is overtaken in any trespass, you who are spiritual restore such a one in a spirit of gentleness, considering yourself lest you also be tempted."*

Don't swim with sharks! Don't whet your appetite by preying on the weak.

Remember what Ma said, "Be careful not to burn bridges. They may be the same planks you'll need to cross back over one day."

Set aside your personal agenda and God will take what seems to an ordinary day and turn it into an extraordinary adventure.

STOP at a busy intersection ***LOOK*** beyond the dirty jeans, the oily hair and the scruffy beard. ***LISTEN*** for the heartbeat of God.

223

CPSIA information can be obtained at www.ICGtesting.com
Printed in the USA
LVOW080144090713

341932LV00002B/5/P